INNOVATION
IS A STATE OF
MIND

INNOVATION
IS A STATE OF
MIND

SIMPLE STRATEGIES TO BE MORE
INNOVATIVE IN WHAT YOU DO

JAMES O'LOGHLIN

WILEY

First published in 2016 by John Wiley & Sons Australia, Ltd
42 McDougall St, Milton Qld 4064
Office also in Melbourne

Typeset in 11.5/13.5 pt ITC Garamond Std by Aptara, India

© What's Going on There Pty Ltd 2016

The moral rights of the author have been asserted

National Library of Australia Cataloguing-in-Publication data:

Creator:	O'Loghlin, James.
Title:	Innovation is a State of Mind: simple strategies to be more innovative in what you do / James O'Loghlin.
ISBN:	9780730324393 (pbk.)
	9780730324409 (ebook)
Notes:	Includes index.
Subjects:	Creative ability in business.
	Creative thinking.
	Organizational change.
	Organizational effectiveness.
	Technological innovations
	Success in business.
Dewey Number:	658.1

Cover design by Wiley

Cover image by Matthew Martin

Printed in Singapore by C.O.S. Printers Pte Ltd

10 9 8 7 6 5 4 3 2 1

Disclaimer

The material in this publication is of the nature of general comment only, and does not represent professional advice. It is not intended to provide specific guidance for particular circumstances and it should not be relied on as the basis for any decision to take action or not take action on any matter which it covers. Readers should obtain professional advice where appropriate, before making any such decision. To the maximum extent permitted by law, the author and publisher disclaim all responsibility and liability to any person, arising directly or indirectly from any person taking or not taking action based on the information in this publication.

CONTENTS

ABOUT THE AUTHOR

James O'Loghlin is an author, speaker, comedian and broadcaster. After finishing university he began work as a corporate lawyer, but soon realised he'd made a mistake and moved into criminal law, which he practised for six years. At the same time he was performing stand-up comedy, appearing regularly on television and radio, and doing shows all over the country.

James started working for ABC local radio in 2001 and hosted the NSW and ACT evening show from 2002 to 2007. From 2009 to 2014 he hosted the national Sunday evening show.

Between 2005 and 2011 James hosted more than 300 episodes of *The New Inventors* on ABC TV.

He now speaks to and works with organisations to help them to become more innovative.

James has written six previous books, including *Umm... A Complete Guide to Public Speaking, How to Balance Your Life* and two novels for children, *The Adventures of*

Sir Roderick the Not-Very Brave and *Daisy Malone and the Blue Glowing Stone.*

He lives in Sydney with his wife and three daughters.

You can get in touch with James via his website, www.jamesologhlin.com, or on Twitter @Jamesologhlin.

PREFACE

In 2004 the ABC decided to reboot *The Inventors*, a television show that had run from 1970 to 1982, and call it *The New Inventors*. The concept was simple. Each week, three inventors would bring their invention into the studio, explain what it was and demonstrate how it worked. Three judges would pass comment, and a host would try to make it all run smoothly.

I was presenting an evening radio show for the ABC at the time and was asked to audition for the role of host. I was pretty motivated, both because I liked the idea of working with lots of people who had created something entirely new, and also because we had just bought a house and become the proud owners of a large mortgage. I was lucky enough to get the job and over the next eight years met and worked with over a thousand Australian inventors and innovators who had thought of, and created, all sorts of things — from a fence that collapses itself onto the ground when there's a flood so it doesn't get damaged, to a system that allows deaf students to instantly read what their teacher is saying in the classroom, to a house gutter that empties itself of leaves, to an outdoor café table that auto-adjusts to any uneven surface so its legs don't wobble, to a wood substitute made from plastic waste … and hundreds more.

Each week before the show we would have a long rehearsal in which we worked out the best way to show viewers how the inventions worked. I used every spare moment to quiz the inventors about how they had come up with their ideas, developed them and turned them into reality. I did this both because I wanted to discover interesting information that we could use on the show, but also because I was becomingly increasingly curious about how people come up with new and better ways of doing things.

I wanted to find out how inventors and innovators differed from the rest of us. They lived in the same world as the rest of us, yet somehow they seemed to see opportunities that the rest of missed, and then take advantage of those opportunities. How did they do it? Was innovation a talent that only some people were born with, or was it something we could all learn to do?

What was their point of difference? Were innovators more intelligent than me? More creative? Did they have a special, extra bit of brain that I lacked? Because if they did, that would let me off the hook. If, to be an innovator, you had to be born with some talent that I didn't have, then I wouldn't have to beat myself up for not dreaming up a great innovation. Instead, I could just tell myself I wasn't built that way, just as I excused myself from being a great basketball player because I wasn't six foot six. It wasn't my fault.

After *The New Inventors* had been running a few years, I thought I'd worked it out. How were innovators different from the rest of us? As far as I could tell, the answer was that they weren't.

As far as I could see, inventors and innovators *weren't* a special breed of super-human, brilliant, ultra-creative genius. Some of them *were* very smart, but many of the people who had invented really clever things didn't seem to me to be any smarter or more creative than average. They included all sorts of people from all walks of life: builders, nurses, businesspeople, truck drivers, bank managers, tradespeople, students, farmers and many more.

So, I wondered, if it wasn't always some sort of super intelligence and creativity that distinguished inventors and innovators from the rest of us, what was it? How were they able to look at the same world as the rest of us, yet see the possibility of something better?

I began to look closer, and to ask more questions:

- How did innovators identify areas in which there might be an opportunity for innovation?

- Was there some sort of a process that innovators went through to come up with ideas, or did they just hope for a blinding flash of inspiration?

- Did successful innovators have only good ideas? Or did they have *lots* of ideas, some of which were good and some of which weren't? If the latter, how did they separate the good ideas from the not-so-good ones?

- How did they find the determination to go through all the many and difficult stages it took to turn an idea into reality?

- And how did they do it all without going broke?

Before hosting *The New Inventors* I had facilitated and MC'ed events for many organisations. After the show started, I began to get asked to speak on innovation and work with organisations to help them to become more innovative. After doing this for a while, a new set of questions presented themselves:

- Why did so many organisations start out being innovative but then, once they reached a certain size, find innovation more difficult?

- Why did the management of so many organisations continually emphasise the importance of innovation, and yet not encourage and harvest new ideas from the people who knew their business better than anyone—their staff?

- Why did so many employees seem to think that innovation was someone else's job, rather than their own?

- How could an organisation create and maintain a culture that encouraged *everyone* to be innovative, and to be always looking for ways to improve what they did?

- How could management ensure they got access to all the ideas their people had, find the best ones and then implement them in their business?

The New Inventors ran for eight years and ended in 2011. In that time we did over 300 episodes and worked with more than 1000 inventors and innovators. My fascination never dimmed, and neither did my curiosity. As time went on, I began to see patterns: things that many inventors and innovators did that helped them to form their idea and then to develop it.

When I worked with organisations, I noticed that many of them treated innovation as an event, rather than as an essential and ingrained part of their everyday business. For example, they would run an innovation competition where they encouraged everyone to think up an idea to improve the business. It would last for a month, and then it would end.

I also noticed that everyone, from prime ministers and CEOs down, talked about the importance of innovation. The word popped up in many companies' values and mission statements, and many industry conferences and events were themed around innovation. But while there was a near universal acceptance of the *importance* of innovation, it was far less common for anyone to tell you how to actually do it.

The emphasis seemed to be primarily on motivation ('We need to be innovative!') rather than on method ('This is *how* you can be more innovative').

That was understandable. It's easy to tell people that it's important to be innovative. It's a lot more difficult to explain how innovation actually happens. In fact, the idea of a process for innovation—a set of steps that a person or an organisation could follow to create innovation—seems like a contradiction in terms. Didn't innovation occur when people were thinking and operating *outside* systems and processes?

But, I thought, wouldn't it be good if there *was* a process for innovation. Wouldn't it be great if there *were* a set of steps that anyone could follow that would increase the chances that they would come up with a better way of doing things.

I spent my time on *The New Inventors* looking for patterns and common steps that innovators took to identify problems and opportunities, to come up with ideas and to develop those ideas. I was looking for a process for innovation.

So how does that apply to you?

At work, most of us move through our day without constantly being on the lookout for opportunities to be innovative. We spend most of our time simply doing our jobs, rather than thinking about ways in which we could do them *better*. Often, we're not even sure if we are supposed to be innovative. Some companies have innovation departments, so doesn't that mean innovation is *their* job?

Often we assume that the way we do things now is the way they have to be done. We get so used to doing things one way that we forget to think about whether there might be another, better way of doing them. The status quo is a bit like a beanbag. It's comfortable, it's cosy and once you relax into it, it can be hard to find the energy to get yourself out again.

But (unlike most beanbags) the status quo is booby-trapped. While it feels like it will last forever, it won't.

The one constant throughout human history is change. Think about how much your job, your organisation and your industry have changed over the past twenty years, or even the past ten. All of those changes occurred as a result of innovation, and it's not going to stop. So if you think the status quo is here to stay, think again. Whether we like it or not, change is coming and we need to be ready. Now, more than ever before, we need to be innovative.

This book is broadly divided into two parts. The first section sets out a process that will help you be more innovative in what you do. It outlines some methods that will help you to look at everything you do with fresh eyes, identify opportunities for innovation and then take advantage of those opportunities. I also discuss how you can use your ideas and find out which ones are going to work.

The second section focuses on how organisations, big and small, can create a culture that encourages *everyone* to be innovative. It explains how management can ensure that everyone in an organisation sees innovation as part of their job. It outlines a process that will help management to access everyone's ideas to improve the organisation, find the best ones, and then develop and implement them.

The most important starting point, however, is not to let yourself think that innovation is beyond you, or beyond anyone you work with. Innovation isn't something that only some of us can do. It's something we can all do. It's not a gift. Innovation is a state of mind.

INTRODUCTION:
WHAT IS INNOVATION AND WHY DO WE NEED IT?

There are many definitions of innovation. A simple one is this: innovation is thinking of, and then implementing, a better way of doing things. An innovation doesn't have to be something completely new and different. It can be any sort of incremental improvement. It doesn't have to be a new product, or even a new feature of a product. It can be any small advance made to any part of an organisation that makes it better. If you work out a way to make a process or system more efficient, that's innovation. For example, if a process takes a person five minutes to complete, and you work out a way for them to do the same task in four minutes, that's an innovation.

Some people intimidate themselves by thinking that an innovation has to be something *amazing,* like the next smartphone. It doesn't. You are being innovative any time you improve, in some small way, any aspect of the way you do things. A tiny incremental improvement to one part of your business can, over time, create substantial benefits. You don't have to re-*invent* everything. You just need to look out for opportunities to make things a little better. If you keep making small incremental improvements, benefits will follow.

An innovator is someone who introduces a new idea, method or product. You might be thinking, 'Well, that's not me'. Yes, it is. If you ever thought up a game to play when you were a kid, if you have made up a story for your kids, or have written a story (or even part of a story), or improvised an original way to fix something in your home, or come up with a way to improve something you do at work, then you have been an innovator.

Here's a (not very impressive) example of me being innovative. My wife and I used to have a cat who loved sleeping in our bed. I didn't like it much because she snored. The cat, I mean. So I started shutting our bedroom door at night. In response, the cat would jump out the window, run around the outside of the house and then climb in our window. So I decided to shut her in the kitchen/eating area at the back of the house with a cushion to sleep on and no windows open wide enough for her to get out. The entrance to the kitchen was a sliding door. The cat was so keen to get to our bed that she would press her body against the door and slowly slide it open. Tracey was an innovative and determined cat. In response, my innovation, thought up at two o'clock one morning after she had woken me for the third time, was to shove a chopstick between the sliding door and the wall, thus jamming it shut. It wasn't brilliant, but it was an original idea, and it worked.

Innovation has been enormously important in human history. Look around you. Everything you can see that is human-made is a product of human innovation: the chair you are sitting on, your coffee mug, the electric light, your phone, your clothes, this book—they all exist as a result of human innovation.

Innovation is the force that has driven human progress. It is our point of difference as a species. Penguins are doing pretty much what they did a million years ago. They may have evolved a bit, but they haven't innovated much. They still catch fish, raise their kids and try to keep warm the way their ancestors did. Humans, on the other hand, keep warm in very different ways. First we shivered, then we discovered fire and clothes, then we invented houses and fireplaces and insulation and gas and electrical heating.

A word about the difference between innovation and invention. An invention is the creation of a product or the introduction of a process for the first time, whereas innovation can be any sort of incremental improvement to a product or process. For example, the wheel is an invention. If, shortly after its invention, someone noticed that people were getting bored with plain grey wheels and started painting them with red and yellow stripes, that would be an innovation.

Almost every invention has been followed by innovations that improve it. For example, cars today are a lot better than they were fifty years ago. So are sound systems, running shoes and toasters. None of them changed dramatically in a year or two. Rather, a series of incremental innovations have meant that today's versions perform substantially better than their predecessors. Every time I buy a computer it is a bit thinner and lighter than my previous one. Each laptop is only a marginal improvement on the last one, but when I compare the one I have now with the one I had twelve years ago, there is a huge difference.

Humans have gone from using rudimentary stone tools to relying on smartphones, home delivery pizza and coffee machines in only a few thousand years. Whereas our ancestors worried about getting eaten by tigers, we worry about traffic jams, poor mobile coverage and paying electricity bills. Life isn't perfect these days but, thanks to countless inventions and innovations, for most of us it is a lot safer and more comfortable than it has ever been before.

Enough history. What does innovation mean for you and your business?

In the old days you could survive for quite some time without being at all innovative. If you made horseshoes exactly the same way that your parents, grandparents and great-grandparents made them, you would probably get on quite well.

Today, the pace of change is faster than it has ever been before. Many industries that have done things pretty much the same way for decades, even centuries, have had to reinvent themselves as a result of the digital revolution.

For example, for the past couple of thousand years if you wanted to buy something you went to the shop or the market. Now, suddenly, you don't have to. You can browse and purchase on your phone, and a few days later the thing you bought will arrive on your doorstep. Online retail is a fantastic innovation for the consumer, but is totally disruptive for the retail industry. Retailers must adapt or be left behind.

Nowadays there are very few industries in which you can be confident that things will still be done the same way in ten years' time. Even traditional industries like agriculture are changing.

Being a custodian of knowledge used to be enough. A couple of hundred years ago, if you were the person in your community who knew how to make candles, that would pretty much guarantee you a career. However, now that the internet has democratised knowledge and everyone can find out almost anything they want by googling it, simply possessing knowledge is less valuable. What is more important is how we *apply* that knowledge in a creative and innovative way.

The problem is that no matter how well you do things now, if you keep doing them the same way, then sooner or later you will be left behind. Someone will think up a better way of doing what you are doing, and then your business will be vulnerable.

To put it another way, today's cutting-edge best practice very quickly becomes tomorrow's fax machine.

When the fax machine came onto the market in the 1980s, it was like magic. Suddenly, everything that was on a piece of paper *here* could instantly be transferred to a piece of paper all the way *over there*! It blew my mind! Now, just 35 years later, fax machines are virtually obsolete. That's a pretty quick turnaround.

How many of the things you do today in your business, or in your job, will be done the same way in twenty years' time? In ten years? In five? Whatever job you have, whatever industry you are in, whatever business you are a part of, it is almost certain that much of it will be done differently ten years from now.

We don't know *how* things will change, but we can safely predict that they *will*, because that is what has always happened in human history. We know that change is coming, and yet most of the time we act as if it is not. Most of us spend lots of time *doing* our job, but very little time thinking of, and developing, innovative ways to do it *better*.

Many people have inboxes, diaries and to-do lists that are so full that they often feel they don't have a spare minute to think. They work hard doing everything that needs to be done to keep their business going *today*, but ignore the need to innovate to ensure they are ready for tomorrow.

Innovators don't do that.

Innovation is how we get to the future. It's how we make it. And if *you* don't do it, someone else will. Of course change can be uncomfortable, but the alternative is worse. If we duck the challenge of change, then opportunity passes us by.

It's not that hard to make the case that innovation is important. If you agree that it is, then you have the *motivation* to try to find better ways of doing things. But what you really need is a *method*.

The *why* is easy. It's the *how* that's tricky.

PART I
A PROCESS FOR INNOVATION

Let's get to the *how*.

◻ How do innovators identify opportunities for innovation?

◻ Once they have identified an opportunity for innovation, how do they take advantage of it?

◻ How do they think of innovative ideas?

◻ Once they have an idea, how do they grow it into something usable?

◻ How do they asses and test ideas, and work out which ones are going to be worth implementing?

There are several things that innovators do better than the rest of us. The good news is they aren't things that only some people can do. They are things we can all learn to do.

The first thing innovators do better than the rest of us is that they think.

Chapter 1

THINK

Innovators think.

I don't mean they are all super-intelligent. I mean they regularly spend time trying to think of ways of making things better.

'But wait a minute,' you might reply. 'I spend my whole day thinking. That's why I'm so tired and crabby every evening.'

Do you, though? How much of your day do you spend thinking, and how much of it do you spend reacting, responding, coping, going to meetings, arranging meetings, managing others, being managed, reading emails, answering emails, talking on the phone, retrieving and replying to messages on your mobile that you missed because you were on your landline, retrieving and replying to messages on your landline that you missed because you were on your mobile...?

How often do you get to the end of the day and realise that you have not had one spare moment to think?

Usually when I ask groups this question, pretty much everyone in the room puts up their hand.

Innovators don't let that happen. They don't treat innovation as something they do if they have time after they have finished all their work. They realise that innovation *is* the work.

Prioritise thinking

When I say that innovators think, I mean they prioritise thinking. They realise that thinking is important, so they make sure they do it. They spend time—often a bit of time each day—thinking about how to make things better. They don't do it when they are tired. They pick a time of the day when their mind is fresh and they try to work out how to solve a problem or take advantage of an opportunity.

I'm not suggesting you spend hours each day staring out the window dreaming of a better world. What I am suggesting is that, while you continue to spend most of your day dealing with today's problems, you also invest a small part of your time—just 1 or 2 per cent of each day—thinking about how to change the things you do to make them better. If you work between eight and nine hours a day, that's about ten minutes a day.

If you accept that your job, your business and your industry will all continue to change, then isn't spending 100 per cent of your time focused on today, and none of it on getting ready for tomorrow, over-prioritising today at the expense of tomorrow?

Innovation always starts with the same thing: it starts with someone having an idea. No matter how sophisticated your software and how clever your systems, ideas come from only one place. They come from us. And the more time we spend trying to think of ideas, the more likely we are to have them. So, if you want to be innovative in your work or in the rest of your life, the first thing to do is to accept that you are going to have to do some thinking.

I once asked an inventor how he came up with his idea and he began by saying, 'Well, I was doing my thinking and...'

'Wait a minute,' I interrupted. 'What do you mean, "doing your thinking."?'

He explained that each day he would make sure he spent some time thinking about how to solve a problem or take advantage of an opportunity. He didn't always come up with something, but often he did.

He thought about thinking in a similar way to how we think about exercise. If you exercise your body every day, you will get fitter and stronger. He figured that if you exercised your brain every day and practised thinking, you'd get better at that too.

The first step to being more innovative is to commit to spending more time thinking about how you can improve the way you do things.

The problem is that it is now harder to find time to think than it has ever been before.

It wasn't that long ago that you could expect several quiet spots in your day during which there really wasn't anything much else to do but think. It might be when you were walking to the train station, or waiting for the bus, or having lunch in the park, or walking from one building to another, or in a taxi, or walking the dog, or at home when there was nothing good on television and you were too tired to read a book. It was often in those moments that your mind would turn, without prompting, to problems and opportunities and begin to puzzle over them...and sometimes, just sometimes, an idea would germinate.

It didn't necessarily happen because you were mad keen on spending every spare moment you could in methodically working your way through a problem. It was more that there wasn't actually anything else to do, so if your mind wasn't kept active in some way you'd get bored.

So our minds would wander, and we would free-associate and ruminate and analyse and imagine and maybe even overhear someone say something that sparked a thought that led to an idea...that sometimes became the beginning of something.

That's less likely to happen when you are checking your Twitter feed.

Nowadays those quiet moments happen far less frequently. Instead, we pull out our phones and fill every spare moment by reading and answering emails, texting, doing work, checking Facebook and Twitter, watching YouTube, playing games, listening to music … and so on.

I'm no Luddite. I'm as connected and plugged in as the next person, and of course the communications revolution has brought great advantages. On the bus we can now get some work done, or be entertained by music or a movie or by shooting for the next level of 'DoomFinder 8'. As a result, though, we have far fewer quiet moments for reflection, and those are often when new ideas come to us.

Remember the story of Isaac Newton and the apple tree. Seeing an apple fall from the tree set off some thoughts about the nature of gravitational force. If he'd been answering emails, checking the news or listening to Mozart's latest single on iTunes, his mind would probably have been too cluttered for him even to notice the apple.

The way you use technology is up to you. You control your own access to it. If we let technology rob us of our thinking time, we can't blame the technology. It's our fault.

If, by the end of this book, you have come to the view that you should spend more time thinking, then give yourself the opportunity to do so. Don't jump onto your phone every time you have a quiet moment. Don't crowd your mind by filling it with information that is of no real value to you. If you create some space, then sometimes ideas will come to you when you least expect them, and in the most unlikely times and places.

If you have a problem or an opportunity that you are wrestling with, then go for a walk or a run or sit on a train, and *don't do anything else*. I'm not saying that a solution will necessarily spring into your mind. I'm just saying that the odds are much better than if you spend every spare minute with your mind engrossed in something else. Create some space for your brain to do its work, and see what happens.

So you should spend more time thinking. But what should you think about?'

What do you think about? Identifying opportunities for innovation

The first step toward being innovative is to identify an area in which innovation might take place. Sometimes the areas in which you need to innovate are obvious. For example, with the rise of social media, many companies recognised that they could use these new platforms for marketing purposes. There was clearly an opportunity for innovation there.

If you are aware that your organisation's supply chain is inefficient, or that its customer service is below par, or that your customers or clients are not as loyal as you might like them to be, then you have identified an opportunity for innovation.

Many innovations occur in areas that aren't obvious, however. Of course, *after* the innovation comes into existence, everyone who didn't think of it says, 'Of course! It's so obvious!' Most innovations *are* obvious…after someone else has thought of them. They're not so obvious beforehand. For example, I don't remember anyone in the 1980s saying, 'The problem with my telephone is I can't carry it around in my pocket'. Today the mobile phone *looks* like it must have been an obvious innovation, but back then it wasn't.

So if opportunities for innovation aren't always apparent, how do we identify them?

One useful strategy is to turn the question on its head. Instead of asking where there *is* an opportunity for innovation, instead ask this: where *isn't* there an opportunity for innovation?

The answer is that the only place there is no opportunity for innovation is where something is absolutely perfect—that is, where you are certain that something cannot be improved upon in any way. So look around your business for products and processes that are so good that you are totally confident they will still be exactly the same in ten, twenty or even fifty years. When you find something like that, then there is no opportunity for innovation there.

But are there many things like that? Think about how many aspects of your job, your business and your industry have changed in the past twenty years. How much of what you do now is done in exactly the same way as it was done twenty or thirty years ago? How many aspects of your business are you completely sure will be utterly unchanged in twenty years' time?

Make a note of every part of your job or your business that you think is perfect and cannot be improved upon in any way. You will then have identified the areas in your business where there are no opportunities for innovation.

As for everything else, all the things that are *not* on your list—that is where there *are* opportunities for innovation.

Innovation is not just about the end product or service you supply. You can innovate in any aspect of your business—in your systems and processes, in your marketing, in your supply chain, in how you manage people, in your customer and client service, in how you develop and implement strategy, and everywhere else.

Here are some places to look for opportunities for innovation.

Processes and systems

When you are trying to identify opportunities for innovation, look at all the systems and processes you have in place, and think about whether you can make any of them more efficient.

In almost every workplace there are processes that are so taken for granted that no one even thinks about how efficient or inefficient they are, or whether there might be a better way. It is only when you step back and pull those processes apart that you may be able to see a way to improve them. For example, think about the process of ordering a meal at a restaurant:

1 The waiter shows you to your table and gives you a menu.

2 Sometime later he returns to take your order, but you aren't ready, so he goes away again.

3 You work out what you want to eat.

4 You look around for the waiter.

5 You try to catch his eye.

6 Eventually he comes back and takes your order.

7 He delivers your order to the kitchen.

8 The chef receives the order and cooks your meal.

People have used this process of ordering food for centuries. Most of us take it for granted and never question it, but might there be a more efficient way of doing it?

What if there was a keypad on your table from which you could select your order? Then you wouldn't have to wait until a waiter was free to come to your table. You could order whenever you wanted to. You would just choose what you wanted to eat, press 'Send' and your order would pop up on a screen next to the chef. Or the restaurant could have an app that allowed you to do it on your phone. Instead of nine steps, the new system would have just three:

1 The waiter shows you to your table and gives you a menu.

2 When you are ready you order via keypad or phone.

3 The chef sees the order and cooks your meal.

You wouldn't *have* to use it. You could still talk to the waiter if you wanted to, but for impatient people like me the keypad/app would be great, and it would save restaurants money as they would need fewer staff.

Identify your own systems, pull them apart and think about a way of making them simpler, more efficient and less costly. Perhaps one of your systems has ten steps. Is there a way of reducing that to nine, or eight, or seven?

Interactions with people

You can also be innovative in the way you interact with people. Every time you have a conversation with someone that doesn't go perfectly, it's an opportunity to step back and ask, 'How could I handle that better next time?'

If you have a discussion with a difficult customer, client, manager or colleague, and the conversation doesn't go exactly as you wanted it to, it's tempting to think, 'Well, it wasn't my fault. He was difficult'.

It might be more productive to take a step back, accept that there will always be a (hopefully small) proportion of people you need to deal with who are difficult, and think about how you can handle it better next time.

Identifying that something you are doing is not perfect is the first step toward improving what you do. It means you have identified an opportunity for innovation.

Notice when you feel bad

Feeling frustrated, angry, impatient or irritated at work is a sign that things aren't working as well as they should be. You might get irritated by a system you have to follow or frustrated by how long it takes to do something. In recognising this feeling, you may have stumbled upon an opportunity for innovation. There may be a way to improve the way you do things.

For example, I am impatient when I order a morning coffee and have to wait. If you walk through a business area before 9 am, you'll see dozens of people waiting for coffee at cafés. If you counted up all the people-minutes that workers spend waiting for their morning shot, you would arrive at a very big number.

The fact that I feel impatient when waiting for my coffee to be made means I have identified an opportunity for innovation. What could reduce my impatience? A shorter wait time. What innovation could achieve that?

Now there are apps through which you can order a coffee, which helps, but the big opportunity for innovation is to reduce the amount of time it takes to *make* a coffee. A café seems to need about a minute to make a coffee. I reckon that whoever works out how to reduce that time to thirty seconds is going to make a lot of money.

Here's another one. Getting on a plane takes ages, right? I'm happy to sit on the plane for an hour or two, but I get frustrated by how long it takes to get on and off. So maybe there is an opportunity for innovation there. What about putting the doors in the middle of the plane, rather than at the front? That way, when people get on, half of them will turn left and the other half will turn right, and loading should take about half the time.

Again, I feel frustrated when I get off a plane and find there's a long queue to get a taxi. There are lots of taxis and lots of passengers, but a bottleneck occurs at the point of where the people get in the taxis. One day I was waiting in the queue feeling frustrated and I tried to puzzle out a solution. By the time I got to the head of the queue I had one. It's not that complicated, but it would take a bit of redesign of the loading area. It's kind of hard to describe without a diagram, so I'm going to leave it as an exercise for you. How would you design a way to get people into taxis at the airport more efficiently?

Look out for things that make you feel irritated or frustrated at work. Whenever you identify one, make a note of it. There may well be an opportunity for innovation there.

A method for innovation

1   Once a week, for an hour or two, as you move through your work day, note as many things as you can that you suspect could be done better. Each time you find one, don't try to solve the problem immediately. Just make a note of it. For example, you might suspect that the way your organisation runs its internal communications, or the way it handles customer complaints, or an aspect of its marketing, is less than perfect. Identify as many imperfect things as you can. Be as specific as you can about where you think the problem or opportunity lies.

2   Each day take five or ten minutes and do this: Write down one of the opportunities for innovation that you have identified, at the top of a blank page, and think about how to improve things. Do this when your mind is fresh, not when you are exhausted. Thinking up new ideas is hard, so give yourself the best chance by

doing it when you are alert. Try to make sure you're not interrupted. If you're at your desk, try to ignore your computer and phone. Maybe you should leave the office and go for a walk or sit in a park.

3 Don't put too much pressure on yourself to come up with a great idea straight away. It's not easy! You might feel stupid and frustrated, but don't worry, that's normal. Just try to tease out as many ideas, or even part-ideas, as you can. American scientist Linus Pauling said, 'The best way to have a good idea is to have lots of ideas'. I would add this: 'The best way to have *lots* of ideas is to spend time trying to think of them.'

There's no guarantee that simply by spending time trying to solve a problem or take advantage of an opportunity, you will come up with a usable solution. But it is far more likely than if you *don't* spend time thinking about it.

CHECKLIST 1: LOOKING FOR OPPORTUNITIES FOR INNOVATION

- ☐ Notice things at work that you suspect are not perfect.

- ☐ Examine your systems and processes, especially the ones you take for granted. Could they be improved on or streamlined in any way?

- ☐ Recognise that feeling irritated, frustrated, impatient or angry at work may signal that there is something that could be improved on.

- ☐ Be innovative in how you deal with people.

- ☐ Once you have identified an opportunity for innovation, spend some time thinking about possible solutions.

Habitual thinking

Where do ideas come from? Are there things we can do during our precious thinking time that will help us to come up with better ways of doing things?

When we start trying to think of better ways of doing things and nothing immediately comes to mind, we often feel stupid and frustrated. Where are all the brilliant ideas? How did that flash of inspiration so quickly turn into something banal?

Don't worry. That's normal. Brilliant ideas don't usually leap into your head the moment you start looking for them. Be patient, and be kind to yourself. If nothing comes straight away, don't beat yourself up and tell yourself you're incapable. It takes a while to break out of habitual thinking.

I don't know who coined the term *habitual thinking*, but I first heard it used in a speech by Rosabeth Moss Kanter, a professor of business at Harvard Business School. She said, 'Mindless habitual thinking is the enemy of innovation'.

What is habitual thinking? Imagine you live in the city and you start a new job. Each day for the first week you drive a different way to work to try to discover the quickest route. On Monday you go one way, but you find there's too much traffic. On Tuesday you go another way, but there are too many sets of traffic lights. And so on, until eventually, after five days, you work out the quickest route. So you drive that way every day for the next twenty-three years. Each morning when you get in your car you don't think, 'Hmm, I wonder which way I'll go today?' You just automatically do exactly the same thing you did yesterday. You're not asleep, because you're in control of the car, but you're just going through the motions. You're not questioning or challenging anything about the route you take. Your trip to work has become habitual.

We all spend a lot of each day engaged in habitual thinking.

How much of your day follows a similar routine? When you wake up do you go through pretty much the same series of steps before you leave home? Do you go the same way to work? Do you spend much of the day doing variations on tasks that you have done many times before? Do you eat lunch in the same place? After work, do you go home and do similar things?

If a large part of your day is spent in a habitual way, don't feel bad. It's normal. Often we work out what the best or most efficient way to do something is (like travelling to work) and then we keep doing it that way. It makes sense.

Most of us have days that follow pretty much the same pattern. Even the way we greet people is habitual. Someone says, 'Hi. How are you?' You don't stop, think hard about the question, and then give them an honest answer. Instead, you just say, 'Good, thanks. How are you?'

Much of work is habitual. For instance, when a problem arises for the first time, we work out how to solve it. Imagine a company that makes and sells hammers. One day, for the first time ever, a customer complains that the day after they bought their hammer, it broke. The company would have to work out how to react. Do they give the customer a refund? Do they give them a new hammer? Do they deny liability and insist that one of their hammers would never break so quickly unless it was used incorrectly?

Eventually the company will work out what to do. When, six months later, another customer makes a similar complaint, the company doesn't need to work out how to solve that problem again. They have already done that. They can simply implement the same solution as last time. They now have a 'what to do when customer complains that their hammer broke' procedure.

We create systems and processes to make order out of chaos, and so we don't have to reinvent the wheel every time something happens. That makes sense. It's smart. Organisations work out the best way to deal with recurrent events, then ensure that that procedure is followed every time. As the organisation grows, it implements best practice. If a customer complains, they put the 'complaints-handling procedure' into action. If an employee's parent dies, they implement the 'compassionate leave procedure'. If they are about to introduce a new product, they follow the 'launch a new product' process.

Again, this makes sense, but there is a danger. Habits, processes and systems can lead us to assume that the way things are is the way they have to be. If much of your life is habitual, then eventually you will probably stop questioning what you do, and instead just do it. If you became an electrician, then for the first few months or years you might periodically ask yourself *why* you became an electrician and whether you really *want* to be an electrician. Eventually, however, you would probably get used to the idea that you *were* an electrician and stop asking those questions.

The problem with habitual thinking is that it can lead us to close our minds to other ways of doing things, and cause us to miss opportunities. If we drive the same way to work every day, sooner or later we stop wondering whether there might be a quicker way. If every time a customer complains that their hammer broke we just automatically implement the 'customer complains about a broken hammer' procedure, then sooner or later we stop thinking about whether that is the best way to handle the problem. Instead, this happens:

'Why do you handle customer complaints about broken hammers in that particular way?'

'Well, because that's the way we handle complaints about broken hammers.'

Are there things you do in your business that are justified by similarly circular logic? 'We do things this way ... because this is the way we do them.'

I used to take my kids to play in a big, wild park. There was a playground there but also trees, bushes, fallen logs and a hill for them to explore and muck around in. One day we were there I saw a mother and son in the playground. The boy was playing on the equipment and then, perhaps seeing other kids exploring the rest of the park, he headed off for the trees. He was nearly there when his mum spotted him, quickly chased after him and then pointed him back to the equipment. 'No, no,' she said sternly. 'We play in the playground.'

We all get into the habit of seeing things in a particular way. She equated playing in the park with using the playground equipment, and she was so set in her way of thinking that she didn't see that exploring the rest of the park could also be a fun and valuable experience.

Here's an example of habitual thinking, and seeing beyond it, from *The New Inventors*.

In the first decade of this century there was drought over much of Australia; water restrictions and conserving water were issues that everyone, even people who lived in the city, was aware of. Yet every day we would all turn on hot taps and watch the cold water run down the sink. We would stand there looking at it as it ran down the plughole, every now and then testing it to see if it was warm enough. Finally, when it was, we would put the plug in.

We didn't think we were wasting water. We were just trying to get rid of the cold water that had been sitting in the pipe, so we could get to the hot water we wanted.

Lloyd Linson-Smith realised that every time we waited for the hot water to run we *were* wasting water, and he wanted to find a way to save it. So he invented a thermostat that goes into your water pipe. It measures the heat of the water and, if it is below a certain temperature, it diverts the water to a holding tank. With his invention, when you turn on the hot tap nothing comes out until there is hot water. Then the next time you turn on the cold tap, the cold water you just saved emerges.

We all recognised the need to save water, yet none of us saw the cold water that came out of the hot tap as water we were wasting. We just saw that cold water as something we had to get rid of to get to the stuff we wanted—the hot water. We were all so much in the *habit* of seeing the cold water that came out of the hot tap as an inconvenience that we were unable to see it in any other way.

Somehow Lloyd had been able to step back and see that water differently. Where the rest of us had seen inconvenience, he had seen an opportunity for innovation. When I saw his invention, I had lots of questions:

- How did he manage to identify the cold water coming out of the hot tap as an opportunity for innovation?

- Why hadn't *I* ever recognised that when I turned on a hot tap and watched the cold water run down the sink, I was actually wasting water.

- If I was missing this opportunity for innovation that was right in front of my eyes, what *other* opportunities for innovation was I failing to see?

- Finally, and most importantly, how could I learn to see those opportunities?

It seemed to me that Lloyd had somehow managed to see something that most of us take for granted—cold water coming out of a hot tap—in a different way. He had looked at it with fresh eyes, and managed to break out of habitual thinking.

It's really easy to get set in our ways and to see things in one particular way only. When we do this, without even realising it we are closing our minds to other ways of doing things.

How often do you react to an event automatically and follow a process without questioning whether it is actually the *best* way to handle the matter? That's habitual thinking.

When we start a new job we spend less of our time thinking habitually, because everything is new. We see everything with fresh eyes. Then, as we gain experience and become familiar with the processes and systems, we grow more comfortable. The first time something happens we go, 'Oh no! What do I do now?' The second time we go, 'Oh no! What do I ... wait ... this is the same as happened last week. I know what to do'. The tenth time it happens we roll our eyes, sigh and go, 'Not again'.

What that means is we gradually stop questioning things and instead begin to accept that the way things are is the way they have to be.

We need systems and processes, but we also need to find ways to step back from them. To be innovative, we need to find ways to break out of habitual thinking and start questioning things again. If we don't do that, then we don't see the cold water we waste every time we turn on a hot tap. We just don't see it.

There are almost certainly things that can be improved in your organisation. The first step is to *see* them. I want to outline some specific strategies that you can use to try to break out of habitual thinking.

Eight ways to break out of habitual thinking

Think about the difference between walking the same route you take almost every day (to work, to the train station, to the shop, to the park with your dog) and walking around a place you have never been before.

They are very different experiences. When you walk somewhere you have never been before you look hard and notice everything—you are very aware of your surroundings. It's a different experience from walking to the corner shop and back.

We need to learn to look at our business with fresh eyes, as if for the first time. Here are some ways of doing it.

1. Question everything

Recently one of my kids asked me, 'Why is a chair called a chair?'

Of course, I had no idea. I realised that calling a chair a 'chair' was something I took completely for granted. I had never questioned why we use that word. Children, on the other hand, have relentless curiosity and question everything.

If you want to find opportunities for innovation in your business and to take advantage of them, try to reawaken the curiosity you had as a child. Question everything you do. Pull it all apart and ask, 'Could there be a better way of doing things?'

Some great innovations have come from questioning the unquestionable.

The first wheelbarrow was invented about 2000 years ago. The wheelbarrow is a well-engineered, functional device that is very good for transporting heavy stuff over short distances. The weight is distributed so that it's reasonably easy to push, even with a heavy load. However, when you have to tip the load out, some of this weight comes onto your arms, and after emptying it a few times they start to hurt.

But there's no point in thinking about how to solve that problem, is there, because surely, to empty a wheelbarrow, you have to tip it out? I mean, people have been tipping out wheelbarrows for 2000 years. If there was a better way, then surely someone would have thought of it by now.

John Steber was a builder who came on *The New Inventors* in 2004. He put a hinge on the front of the tray of the wheelbarrow, and some releasable catches on the back of the tray. As you pushed the wheelbarrow along, the clasps held the tray in place. When you reached your destination, you flicked a lever on the handle to release the clasps, stopped, lifted the handles up a little way and then stopped abruptly. The momentum caused the tray to flip forward and empty itself. Using John's wheelbarrow, you can tip out a load without having to lift the handles high and take the weight on your arms. It's a lot easier.

John solved a problem that had been around for 2000 years. He did it by questioning something that no one else had questioned. He asked, 'Is there a way of emptying a wheelbarrow without using your arms to lift up the handles?'

Every day in business we try to answer lots of little questions: How can I get all this work done by lunchtime? How can I make that customer happy? How can I keep my boss satisfied?

Take some time to step back and ask bigger questions, just as John Steber did. Instead of asking, 'How am I going to get this job finished in time?', ask yourself, 'Are all the tools and systems I use to do my job as good as they can possibly be? If they aren't, how can I make them better?'

Question all your tools, all your processes and all your systems. Step back, take a breath and ask, 'Could there be a better way?'

You may often find that the answer is no. But occasionally you will discover an opportunity for innovation, and a way to take advantage of it. If you question fifty things in your business and discover just one or two that can be improved and therefore create ongoing efficiencies, then I would suggest that it is time well spent.

Here's another example of questioning *everything*.

A 14-year-old schoolboy named Suvir Mirchandani, from Pittsburgh in the USA, was trying to think of ways to cut waste and save money in his school as part of a science project. He noticed that students received a lot of paper handouts. He started thinking about the cost of the ink that was used in the printing, and wondered if there might be a way to reduce ink consumption.

He noted the most commonly used letters of the alphabet and set them in four different typefaces: Garamond, Times New Roman, Century Gothic and Comic Sans. Then he enlarged the letters, printed them on separate pieces of paper and weighed each piece of paper. The weight of each piece of paper was identical, so any variation in the weight had to be due to the different amount of ink used by each of the different fonts.

Suvir discovered that switching to Garamond font with its thinner strokes would result in much less ink being used. In fact, he found that if his school district switched all of its printing to Garamond, it would be able to reduce its ink consumption by 24 per cent and save as much as $21 000 each year! He also calculated that if the US Government set all its printing in Garamond it could save $136 million per year, and that if all the US state governments followed suit, that would save an additional $234 million.

All from changing the type font.

Fonts are right there in front of our eyes all the time, and so is the need to be efficient and cut costs. Yet most of us never think much about fonts, much less question their impact on the bottom line.

How many things are there in your business that no one ever questions? Look at them all and see if you can identify some opportunities for innovation.

2. What assumptions are you making?

We all make assumptions about how the world operates. We assume that the sun will come up tomorrow, we assume that it will take about the same amount of time to get to work today as it did yesterday, we assume that if we are in a hurry, we'll get stuck behind a car driving at thirty kilometres per hour.

In business we make assumptions about what customers and clients want, about the best ways to reach them, about how our industry is changing, about the best way to run the business, and many other things.

Assumptions help us make sense of the world, save time and inform our decision making. However, sometimes the assumptions we rely upon become invalid. For example, we used to assume that the quickest way to find out something was to look it up in an encyclopaedia. That is no longer correct.

In retail, up until ten or fifteen years ago it was usually safe to assume that your competitors were those who sold a similar product or service to you *and* were geographically proximate. If you owned the only electronics store in town, then you could assume that that fact alone would pretty much guarantee that as long as you ran a reasonably competent business, you would get the bulk of the business in the area. If you sold electronic goods in Newcastle and they were 10 per cent more expensive than those in Sydney, you could assume that not many people would bother to drive two hours down the highway to get the cheaper goods.

The advent of online retail has meant that those assumptions are no longer valid, because competitors no longer need to be geographically proximate. They can be anywhere.

We used to be able to make certain assumptions about how dissatisfied customers might behave. If they were unhappy with something, they might — *might* — go to the trouble of calling up, or writing a letter to the company, but that would take a fair bit of effort. If they wanted to write, they would have to write a letter, address the envelope, buy a stamp and post the letter, and it was safe to assume that a fair proportion of unhappy customers wouldn't bother to go through all those steps. Even if they did, it was a communication that was only going to be read by those within the company. Of course, a dissatisfied customer might tell a few friends, but they would probably soon forget about it and move on. So, from the company's point of view, the worst thing that could happen wasn't really that bad.

Then social media arrived and those assumptions were no longer valid. Suddenly, if a customer was dissatisfied they could tell the world, and they didn't even have to buy a stamp. They could use Facebook, Twitter, an online forum or all three, and they could do it all while they were waiting for the bus. Worst of all, sometimes they could post a lacerating critique of the company on the company's own website!

The mega-trend was a shift in power from the retailer to the consumer. Retailers who wanted to stay successful had to quickly rid themselves of all their outdated assumptions about how the customer–retailer relationship worked and replace them with more relevant ones.

The assumptions that can safely be made about staff are changing, too. Until relatively recently it was often safe to assume that a high percentage of staff would choose to stay with a company for a long time, provided they were reasonably satisfied with their pay and opportunities for promotion. Now it is much more common for people to move between jobs, and even careers, and there is a greater awareness of work–life balance issues and flexible work arrangements. As a result, some assumptions that employers used to be able to make about their workforce are no longer valid. To be able to employ the best people, employers need to ensure they are not making decisions and developing strategy based on outdated assumptions.

So what assumptions are you making about:

◻ your business

◻ your relationships with your customers

◻ what your customers want

◻ the loyalty of your customers

◻ the best way to market to your customers

◻ the best way to advertise to your customers

◻ your relationships with your suppliers

◻ what your suppliers want

◻ who your competitors are

◻ what your staff want?

One assumption that many of us make is that we assume that the way we do things is the way things should be done. That is, the mere fact that we do things a certain way leads us to assume that it is the *best* way of doing them.

For example: 'We use X as our lawyer, because X is the lawyer we use.'

Maybe X *is* the best lawyer for your organisation. If X has been representing you for fifteen years and knows the company and your history, and has a relationship with you, those are all important factors. But don't *assume* that just because X is your lawyer, that fact alone necessarily means that X is the *best* lawyer for your company. Instead, question your assumptions.

One way to identify and take advantage of opportunities for innovation is to identify your assumptions, and then challenge them. If you find an assumption that doesn't stand up to analysis, then it is time to work on developing a better way of doing things.

The development of inflight entertainment provides an excellent example of an innovation that came about from challenging an assumption. In the old days, air travellers would watch videos on a screen that hung from the ceiling in the middle of the aisle, so everyone had to watch (or not watch) the same thing. The next step was a screen set into the back of the seat in front of you, so you could watch what you wanted when you wanted to. Then the airline started handing out tablets on which you could watch their content.

Throughout this evolution, one assumption was constant: that if you wanted to watch the airline's content, then you had to watch it on the airline's device. And until recently, that was a necessary assumption for the airline to make.

Times change, however.

A few years ago Air Canada, working with IBM, thought about how most people now carried their own device onto the plane, and they decided to challenge the decades-old assumption that the only way to watch the airline's content was on the airline's device.

Why, they wondered, couldn't people watch the airline's content on *their own* device?

They already had an Air Canada app, so they added a feature that allowed wireless streaming of inflight entertainment to the passenger's device. All passengers had to do was download the app before take-off, then they could watch the airline's content on their own computer, tablet or phone.

The benefits for the airline were that they saved the cost of buying, installing and maintaining screens for every seat. Their planes were also lighter because they didn't have a screen installed in the back of every seat, which lowered fuel costs.

It all came from challenging one basic assumption: that if you wanted to watch the airline's content, you had to do it on their device. Once they realised that that assumption, formerly perfectly valid, had become outdated, the rest was pretty logical.

Here's another example of challenging assumptions, from *The New Inventors*.

When people with reduced mobility are confined to bed, they sometimes develop pressure sores, which can be painful and lead to infection and even gangrene. Traditionally, one way of preventing pressure sores has been to move the patient regularly, but that can be painful for the patient and physically demanding for the nurse or carer.

The assumption has been that if a patient is unable to move themselves, then someone else has to move them. That sounds logical, right?

Hannah Piazza had been a nurse for thirty years when, one night, she treated a young woman who was very ill and had to be turned every hour to prevent bedsores. Each time the woman was moved it caused her pain. Hannah decided to try to think of a better way.

What she came up with was a bed that could be programmed to move very slowly in tiny increments in a rocking motion throughout the night, so that, without waking the patient, their weight would be regularly shifted. Instead of a *carer* moving the patient, the *bed* they were lying on moved them.

Hannah had questioned the assumption that a patient had to be moved by another person. Was there another way of approaching the problem? Babies are rocked in the cradle, so why not rock an adult very gently in the same way?

It seems logical now, but the big step was to question the underlying assumption.

CHECKLIST 2: CHALLENGING YOUR ASSUMPTIONS

- ☐ Identify the assumptions you are making about:
  - – your business
  - – your relationships with your customers
  - – what your customers want
  - – the loyalty of your customers
  - – the best way to market to your customers
  - – your relationships with your suppliers
  - – what your suppliers want
  - – who your competitors are
  - – what your staff want.
- ☐ Challenge each one.
- ☐ When you find an assumption that may not be valid, think hard about what opportunities for innovation it may open up.

3. Technology is not always the answer

Innovation begins with an idea and often leads to the creation of a new technology that becomes an accepted part of our lives. The chair, television and the car are all examples of ideas that eventually became new technologies.

Sometimes, however, we can get a little obsessive over new technology. For example, recently we went out to a restaurant and the waiter took our order on an iPad. To be honest, it took a bit longer than usual, but that was okay. It impressed the kids. Curious as to what the next step was, I watched the waiter after he left our table. He walked over to the kitchen, called out to the chef, and then started reading our order from the iPad while the chef grabbed a scrap of paper and scribbled it down.

It was a great illustration of how just *having* the latest technology doesn't achieve anything. It all depends on how you use it.

A lot has been made of ensuring that all high-school students have a computer. Some seem to think that as long as they all have a computer, everything else will fall into place. Just *having* a computer doesn't help a student to learn better. The computer only starts to become useful when new ways of teaching are developed that take advantage of the things a computer can do. What's the point of a student having a computer if they are just using it to do the same things they used to do with a pen and paper? It's not the technology that's most important. It's the method.

The breakthroughs come as teaching methods evolve to take advantage of all the new ways of learning that a computer enables. For example, maybe having computers will allow students to spend less time in the classroom with 25 others and more time learning on their own or in small groups. Instead of always having to hand in a written essay for English or History, they might now be able to hand in something that has more complex audio-visual elements. If a student is at home sick, can they log in and be virtually present in class? How can the fact that students can now collaborate using Skype, email, wikis and instant messaging be used to improve learning?

Some frame it as a debate about technology, but it should be a debate about learning methods. The question isn't, 'How can we make sure that every high-school student has a computer?' The question is, 'How can we improve learning, and what role can computers play in that?'

Technology is no better than the brains that thought of it and the hands that created it. When we are looking for ways to improve our businesses and we identify an opportunity for innovation, these days it can be tempting to think, 'I'm sure if I just wait a bit, some new technology will come along and solve this problem'.

Sometimes that's right. But not always.

Let me give you an example.

Ed Evans won *The New Inventors* Invention of the Year award in the show's final year. He was a cattle farmer who had been injured when one of his cattle charged a stockyard gate that he was behind. The animal charged the gate, and the gate rocketed open and hit Ed hard.

Ed knew that every year many farmers were seriously injured in this way, and that some had even been killed. While they know they shouldn't turn their back on an unlocked gate when there are cattle about, farmers get busy, so every now and again they do. Even if they are facing the gate an animal can move so quickly that there's no time to get out of the way.

Ed started thinking about a solution. He could have looked at new technology; perhaps a gate that automatically shut and locked itself, or an alarm that went off whenever a cow was within five metres of the gate, or even some fancy new type of gate that would open if a human hand released it but not if a cow charged it.

Instead, Ed used a piece of technology that was over 3000 years old: the hinge. He put a hinge in the middle of the gate, so when a cow charged it, instead of the gate slamming straight back and hitting anyone who was on the other side, the hinge would cause the gate to 'break' in the middle and fold back in on itself, like a folding door. This meant that in many circumstances the farmer wouldn't get hit at all. Even if they did get hit, because much of the force would have been absorbed by the gate folding back in on itself, the blow would likely cause less injury.

Cattle farming has been around for about 6000 years, and hinges for about 3000 years. I'm not sure when the first person was injured by a cow charging a gate, but it's clear that the solution to this problem had been technologically available for a long time. It wasn't a lack of technology that stopped this problem being solved. It was a lack of innovative thinking.

Here's another example. At conferences, it's always hard to get people back into the room on time after morning and afternoon tea. It's not because they're evil or slack. It's just that they get involved in conversations and want to keep talking. Event organisers try loudspeaker announcements and playing music, but people often ignore them. If it hasn't already been done, no doubt someone will soon try sending all the delegates a text message saying, 'Please come back in! We're about to start!' The most effective way to get everyone back inside doesn't rely on any new technology. The most effective way is for someone to walk around ringing a little bell and looking people in the eye. It works because, while it's easy to ignore a disembodied sound coming from a loudspeaker (or a text message), it's hard to ignore a real person without feeling you are being rude.

Maybe there are some challenges, or opportunities, in your business that you are assuming can only be solved by new technology. Perhaps that assumption is holding you back from really examining the problem closely, and looking as hard as you can for a solution that you can implement with technology that already exists.

When you do invest in new technology, remember the waiter with the iPad, and high-school children and their computers. Keep asking yourself if you are using the technology in the smartest way possible, and taking full advantage of everything the technology can help you to do.

4. Reframe the question

Sometimes, when trying to come up with an innovative way of doing things, we get stuck. It happens to everyone. We identify a problem to be solved, we do some quality thinking and we come up with … nothing. Every solution we think of has a fatal flaw, and as our frustration mounts we begin to think this problem is one that simply does not have a solution.

Sometimes we're right. Some problems *don't* have a solution.

When you think you have found a problem that has no solution, try reframing the question. That is, take the question you have been trying to answer and ask it again in a slightly different, perhaps slightly less ambitious, way. Often this can open up some new ways to explore an answer.

Here's a great example from the world of self-combusting hay bales.

If hay bales get hot enough, they can spontaneously combust. On hot summer days the temperature in the middle of a hay bale can rise to the point where the bale bursts into flame. Han Van Wyc read about a farmer whose haystack caught on fire; the fire spread and caused the farmer $100 000 worth of damage. Han decided to try to think of a solution. He asked this question:

'How can I stop hay bales from overheating?'

It was the logical question to ask. If he could stop them getting too hot, then they wouldn't ignite. He tried to think of a way of preventing the inside of the bale from going over 60 degrees Celsius, when combustion can occur. Would shading do it? But the bales could be anywhere on the farm. What about watering? Again, there were practical problems.

Whichever way he looked at it, he came up against problems. Perhaps it was one of those problems that just didn't have a solution.

Then Han did something brilliant: he reframed the question.

He started to look at the problem in a different way. If he couldn't work out a way to *stop* the hay bales overheating, then maybe he could work out a way to let the farmer know *when* they were overheating. What if he could develop a system that somehow warned the farmer when the temperature inside the bale was approaching 60 degrees Celsius? If the farmer knew when one of their bales was getting dangerously hot, then they could just carefully pull apart that one bale to allow the heat to dissipate, and all would be well.

That wouldn't be quite as good as inventing something that would *prevent* the bales from overheating, but it would still be pretty useful.

This is what Han invented. He took a hollow pipe and in one end he introduced a plug made from an alloy that melts at 60 degrees Celsius. Behind the plug was an orange rod. You push the end of the pipe with the alloy plug and the orange rod into the middle of the bale, and leave the other end of the pipe sticking out of the bale so that the pole points slightly downwards. When the bale gets dangerously hot, the alloy plug melts, which allows the orange rod to slide down the inside of the pipe until it sticks out of the side of the bale, clearly visible to anyone passing.

All the farmers need to do is to regularly drive past all their hay bales and look to see if any have an orange rod hanging out of them. If they find one that does, they know it's getting too hot, so they quickly (but carefully) pull it apart before it combusts.

The important point is this. Han got stuck. He couldn't solve his problem. He could have given up, but instead he reframed the question to make it slightly less ambitious. Yes, it would have been better if he could have found a way to *stop* the hay bales from overheating, but failing that, the next best thing was to think up a way of finding out *when* they were overheating.

If you have identified an opportunity for innovation, or a problem to be solved, and you get stuck, then try to reframe the question you are asking. Perhaps there is another, slightly less challenging question you can ask that will still lead you to a useful solution.

For example, imagine a retail company was trying to answer this question: 'How can we increase our online sales via our website?'

Say they came up with a number of ideas, but for one reason or another none of them were successful. They could decide to give up, or instead they could reframe the question. Instead of asking, 'How can we increase online purchases?' they could ask, 'How can we get more people to look at our website, and stay on it for longer?'

If the company could get more customers to look at their website, and increase the time customers spent on it, that might well lead to an increase in online purchases.

Coming up with strategies to get more customers to look at the website, and to stay on it for longer, isn't quite as good as devising a strategy to increase online purchases, but it's still pretty good, *and* it's a lot easier to achieve. The company could upload entertaining videos, interesting information, competitions, themed games and quizzes. They could ensure that attractive offerings for online purchase were displayed near the entertaining content, and see if that led to an increase in purchases.

Reframing the question is something we often do without even realising we are doing it. Remember when you were in high school and had a crush on someone? The question you might have asked yourself initially was, 'How can I get that person to be my girlfriend/boyfriend?' But that was probably too ambitious, so you reframed the question to one that was a little easier to achieve: 'How can I get her/him to go on a date with me?' Sometimes even that question was too audacious, so you reframed it again to, 'How can I get her/him to notice me?'

In your business, look for problems you have been unable to solve, or opportunities you have been unable to take advantage of, and see if you can reframe the question that you have been asking in a different, slightly less ambitious, way. If you can't work out a way of getting *everything* you want, that doesn't mean you should give up. There may well be a way to 80 per cent, or even 50 per cent, of what you want.

5. The solutions might be right in front of your eyes

Today we are exposed to more information than ever before. To prevent ourselves becoming overwhelmed, we try to organise all this information by creating something like a filing system in our brain. Each bit of new information that comes in is unconsciously filed away in the appropriate place. For example, if you discover you are putting on weight, that piece of information gets filed under 'health' (or, if you are vain, 'appearance'). If a new supermarket opens up down the road, you file that under 'shopping information'.

That all makes sense, but sometimes the silos we create are so rigid that they stop us from connecting different pieces of information in ways that might help us to find solutions to problems. Breaking down the silos, and looking for connections between different pieces of information, can help us to come up with some unexpected and useful ideas.

Here's an example of how silos can prevent us from solving problems. The other day I was looking for a book, *I, Claudius* by Robert Graves. When I was a kid I watched the television series and read the book, and I decided I wanted to re-read it. I looked through our two bookcases, but couldn't find it. Increasingly frustrated, I searched them again, and then looked everywhere else I thought a book might have got buried. Eventually I gave up and went back to working on my computer in my office.

That evening I told one of my kids that I had lost the book, and she said, 'I've seen that book. Your computer monitor is sitting on it'.

At my desk I plug my laptop into a monitor, but the monitor is a bit low so I put three books under it to make it higher. The books are facing spine out, so the entire time I was sitting at my desk feeling irritated about not being able to find *I, Claudius*, it was literally right in front of me. I was looking straight at it.

Why didn't I see it?

In my mind, books belong in the bookcase. If the book I was looking for wasn't in the bookcase, then the only other thing that could have happened, I figured, was that someone had left it lying around after they had read it. I only thought of the book in one way—as something you read.

That piece of information—that a book is something you read—was so rigidly ingrained in my mind that I simply didn't see the objects that my monitor was balancing on as books. Because they weren't doing what books were supposed to do then, according to my information filing system, they weren't books. They were things I sat my monitor on to make it higher.

Kids, however, often haven't yet learned about putting every piece of information in a little box, so my daughter's thinking was more flexible.

Sometimes the solution is right in front of us. We just need to learn how to see it.

Here's an example from *The New Inventors*. Lincoln Morris was an HSC student who had a friend whose family were trying to farm bass in a dam. Bass eat tadpoles, small fish, insects and other small creatures, and his friend's family were trying to find a viable food source for the bass they were farming.

Lincoln's friend had told him that when playing tennis at night he had seen moths clustering around the lights. He wished there was a way to use the moths to feed his bass.

Lincoln thought about this and then got to work. He built a pontoon, shaped like a small catamaran, and from it hung long UV lights about 20 centimetres above the water. When the lights are turned on and the pontoon is pushed into the water at dusk or after, the insects cluster around the lights and the fish swim to the surface, stick their heads out of the water and eat them. The fish now have a plentiful source of food.

Lincoln and his friend had come up with the innovation by putting together two bits of information that the rest of us would never have thought to associate:

1 Insects are attracted to light.

2 The fish like to eat insects.

Once those two bits of information were next to each other, the solution became clear; put light near the water, and the insects would flock to it. The solution to the problem was right in front of their eyes, and their minds were flexible enough to allow them to see it. Sometimes simply putting two different pieces of information next to each other can suggest a solution to a problem.

6. Is the answer in your data?

Today we can access more data than ever before. Used the right way, analysis of that data can offer you great insights and help you to be innovative in what you do. Use data the wrong way, and you can find yourself drowning in numbers, graphs and spreadsheets.

So how do you get the insights without drowning in the data?

A lot has been said about 'big data'. Data itself does nothing. It is only *potentially* useful. What is important is the quality of our analysis of it. Rather than jumping into the data in the hope that an insight will 'appear', often a better strategy is to first come up with a specific question you want an answer to.

Say your question is, 'Why aren't more people making purchases via our website?' You can use data to discover:

- how many people are visiting your website
- where they are from
- whether they are existing customers or others
- what areas of the website they are visiting
- how long they are staying there
- what areas of the website they *aren't* visiting.

Using the data to find answers to these questions may shed light on what people are doing and not doing on your website, why more purchases aren't being made and some strategies to address that.

Point Defiance Zoo & Aquarium in Tacoma in the US used their data to find the answer to a very specific question. They knew there was a relationship between attendance at their zoo and the weather. What they didn't know was the *exact* relationship.

With help from IBM and the National Oceanic and Atmospheric Administration, they analysed their past attendance figures and weather data and were able to come to a better understanding of how the two factors interacted. Now that they knew more about this relationship, they were able to make better decisions about rostering staff. If they knew that Monday was going to be sunny, they could roster more staff in the expectation of getting lots of people. If it was going to rain on Tuesday, they could roster fewer staff.

Remember how it began. They knew there was a relationship between two factors—the weather and attendance—but they didn't know exactly what that connection was, so they used data to discover more about it, and as a result were able to make better decisions and use their resources more efficiently.

Are there some relationships between different factors in your business that you are aware of but unable to evaluate or quantify accurately? Is your business seasonal? Are there peaks and troughs in which you can't quite see a pattern? Could an analysis of your data help you to see patterns that you are currently unaware of?

Another American zoo, Cincinnati Zoo and Botanical Garden, wanted to know how their visitors spent money during their visit, so they analysed data from all their food outlets. One of the things they looked at was the times of day that visitors bought food. They already knew sales tailed off after 3 pm, and as a result they started to close some of their food outlets after that time. However, from their analysis they discovered that there was a spike in ice-cream sales in the hour before closing time. That makes sense. Families walk around, they have lunch, they walk around some more, then toward the end of the day the kids get tired and start complaining. To save the day, Mum or Dad quickly suggests an ice cream. Everyone cheers up, and the ice cream gives the kids just enough energy to make it back to the car.

Once the zoo had that insight, the change it suggested was obvious: they knew to keep all their ice-cream outlets open right up to closing time.

Remember, they were looking at something specific: how and when their visitors spent money. The more they knew about that, the more likely they would gain an insight that would allow them to improve the way they did things. Remember also that once they had the information (ice-cream sales peak toward the end of the day), the course of action became obvious (keep ice-cream outlets open right up until the zoo closed).

So, when analysing data, try to be specific about the information you want to obtain. What questions about your customers, or your business, do you want to know the answer to? Work out the questions you are going to ask before you jump into the data.

Perhaps you can use data to get a clearer picture of exactly what it is that your customers want. Upworthy is a media site dedicated to finding, writing and producing news content. They wanted to learn what factors influenced people's decision either to read a story right to the end or, having lost interest, to click away partway through. They analysed their website traffic data to find how long people stayed on stories, and from that information they were able to work out at what point in the story readers lost interest and left.

They discovered that a story containing humour was likely to keep people reading for longer. Again, once they had the insight, the course of action it suggested was obvious. Now, even in serious stories, they try to include humour.

They also learned that suspense keeps people reading, so now they try to structure their stories in such a way that people want to know what is going to happen next.

By collecting and analysing 'attention minutes' data, each week they can see which stories successfully engage readers and which don't. When stories don't engage readers, they can see where the story lost them and work out how they could do it better next time.

Are there insights you can gain about your own clients and customers from analysing their behaviour? Are you able to find out when they lose interest, or become disengaged?

There are lots of organisations that could use data to improve what they do. For example, schools want their teachers to be as good as they can be. In fact, we all want that. But how often do educators collect data from the people who know more about their teachers than anyone else, the students? Many schools rarely or never ask students for feedback on their teachers, and yet that information could be incredibly useful in helping teachers improve.

Getting the feedback wouldn't be hard. At the end of the year students could be asked to rate their teacher out of 5 in different areas; patience, control of the class, how much they shout, and so on. Of course, you would need to be careful when interpreting the answers of ten-year-olds, but if 80 per cent of the class said they thought their teacher shouted too much, that would surely be useful feedback for the teacher to have.

When I was at school I thought the worst times were when I was bored. Back then I thought, and I still think now, that if a large proportion of students are bored, something isn't working properly. Schools could gather data on boredom, and then try to eliminate it, in this way:

1 Ask students to list the parts of the school week in which they get bored. Is it in assembly, maths, history ...? Encourage them to be honest.

2 Whenever a part of the week is identified as being boring by more than 25 per cent of students, there is an opportunity for innovation.

3 The next step would be for teachers to think about how they can make that part of the week more engaging for students (while ensuring, of course, that the students learn).

4 Once there are no longer any parts of the week in which more than 25 per cent of students are bored, repeat the process, but this time act whenever there is a boredom rating of more than 15 per cent.

What can your data tell you about your customers and clients? What can it tell you about what they want? And about what they don't want? Do the insights you gain into your customers and clients suggest any changes you can make that will make your business more attractive to them?

CHECKLIST 3: USING DATA

- ☐ What data do you have access to?

- ☐ What are some questions that you would like to know the answer to? (For example, Cincinnati Zoo wanted to find out how and when visitors spent money during their visit.)

- ☐ Can the data you have access to help you to answer those questions?

- ☐ If so, what insights can you obtain from the data?

- ☐ Once you have those insights, what changes do they suggest you might make?

7. Think like a customer or client

It's easy to say that your business is 'customer facing', that it 'focuses on the end user' and so on, but how often do you actually spend an hour in the shoes of one of your customers or clients? The best way to make sure that your business is as customer-friendly as it can be is to regularly experience your business *as a customer*.

For example, a bookstore owner once told me that once a week he entered his own shop as a customer. When he came in and looked around as a regular shopper, he found that he would often think of a way to make some sort of improvement to the layout of his store. Even though he was in the store every day, he gained these insights into how he could improve his customers' experience only when he stood in their shoes.

Sometimes in business all the processes and systems we use seem to make sense, and it is only when we experience them from the customer's point of view that we recognise they could be better.

I once met an executive of a large retail food chain who said he visited customers at home and looked in their cupboards and their fridge for insights into how they shop. Then he went shopping with them. He was committed to getting as close as he could to his customers so he could understand how and why they made decisions.

Here's an example of a process that looks good on paper, but as soon as you experience it as a customer you realise it's terrible.

A few years ago my credit card expired. The bank sent me a new card, and then I had to try to remember all my direct debits and change them over or else my payments would fail. If I forgot to inform the insurance company of my new card details, they would eventually email or ring me, and I would apologise and give them the new card number.

(Now this process seems to occur automatically, which is a good innovation.)

One of my direct debits was to a charity. The month after I got my new credit card they rang me and said, 'You missed your payment'. Their choice of words really irritated me. My donations were voluntary, but they made it sound like I owed them money.

What they should have done was to thank me for my previous donations and then draw my attention to the fact that the previous payment hadn't gone through. Instead, they used a script that was appropriate for a business, but not for a charity. The relationship between a business and a customer is very different from the relationship between a charity and a donor. If they had put themselves in their customer's shoes, they would have realised that donors don't like to be treated like debtors.

Here's a wonderful example of thinking like a customer. For several years I hosted the Australian Clean Technologies Competition, an Australian Government initiative that offered mentoring and other assistance to new technology companies, including many whose innovation involved a better or more efficient use of energy. There were some amazing entries, including a plant fertiliser made from recycled glass and a technology that harvested the heat from the sunlight that came through office, home and even car windows, then converted the heat into energy that was used to power the air conditioner.

The program was designed as a competition and the further through the competition an innovation progressed, the more assistance it got. In 2012 the competition was won by a company that supplied lighting to businesses.

What's so innovative about that? Quite a lot, actually.

A few years earlier, they had realised that the lighting industry was changing. Ever since electric lighting had been around, people had pretty much wanted only one thing from a lighting company, and that was lighting products.

This century, however, electricity prices have gone up and people have started to become more concerned about the environment. Suddenly people want more than light from a lighting company. They also want to reduce the amount of money they are spending on electricity, and to reduce the amount of energy they use—to go green (or at least, to be seen to be going green).

Those who started enLighten figured that these two new trends—rising electricity prices and increased awareness of the environmental cost of electricity—were unlikely to be reversed. So they started to think about what they could do for clients to help them to reduce their electricity bills. They realised that many workplaces kept lights on all the time in areas where there were people only *some* of the time—for example, in car parks, corridors, toilets, stairwells and fire escapes.

Many people remember a parent nagging at them to turn the light off when they left a room. Yet companies were spending lots of money lighting areas even when there were no people in them.

EnLighten saw the beginning of a trend toward increased demand for lighting products that saved electricity. They calculated that the trend was going to continue and grow, then they thought like their customers. If electricity was going to keep getting more expensive, then what sorts of products would their customers want? Clearly, products that helped them to save electricity and cut costs. How could businesses do that? By doing what kids are told to do at home: 'Turn the lights off when you leave the room.'

Once enLighten had worked out what their customers were going to want, all they had to do was to put themselves in a position to supply it.

EnLighten developed a suite of products that businesses could use to reduce their electricity bills while still properly lighting areas when there were people using them. These included motion sensors that would switch lights on and off when a person arrived and left a room or area, as well as timers and dimmers. You have probably been in a toilet, stairwell, corridor or car park where such products are used.

Here's another great example of thinking like a customer. Chemists, or pharmacists, sell healthcare products— medicine, vitamins, shampoo, mosquito repellent and so on. Why, then, did I see one that sold toy buckets and spades? That's got nothing to do with healthcare!

The answer is that the people in that chemist were thinking like their customers. The chemist was near the beach. They sold sunscreen, probably a fair bit of it. They also sold sunhats. They realised that if their customers wanted sunscreen and the beach was only five minutes' walk away, then those customers might also want a beach hat. And they might be going to the beach with their kids and want some beach toys. So, they figured, customers would come in for sunscreen, and then see the hats and the buckets and spades and maybe buy them too.

What they did was to work out what other things their customers might want, and then supply them. If their customers wanted sunscreen, then there was a good chance that they might want a hat and beach toys too. The fact that plastic toys aren't what a chemist traditionally sells didn't matter.

If a customer or client is doing business with you, what else, apart from the goods or service that you sell, might they be after? If you supply running shoes, then your customers might also want sweat bands, energy drinks and a cap. If you supply plumbing services, your customers might also need a handyman. If you supply airline flights, your customers might want a hire car or accommodation at the other end. Customers and clients want their life to be as easy as possible. Generally, that means dealing with as few companies that supply goods or services as possible. So make life easy for them: work out what else your customers might want, and supply that too. It doesn't necessarily mean that if you are a plumber you should also become a handyman. Instead, you could find a good handyman, and enter an agreement with him or her whereby you try to scout work for each other.

Put yourself in your own customers' or clients' shoes, and think hard about the answers to these questions:

- What do your customers really want?
- How is what they want changing?
- What will your customers want more of in four years' time?
- What will they want less of in four years' time?
- How is your relationship with your customers changing?
- How might it change more in the next four years?
- What trends do you see in your industry?
- Which of those trends are likely to continue and to grow over the next five to ten years?
- What new demands will those trends create?
- What products and services will satisfy those demands?
- What can do you do to put yourself in a position to provide those products and services?

Try to pay more than lip-service to thinking like a customer. Experience as many parts of your business as you can from the point of view of your customers. Go into one of your stores and buy something. What were the good parts of the experience? What were the bad parts?

Telephone your business with a problem that a customer might have and see how easy or difficult it is to get your problem solved. How long were you put on hold for? Was the first person you spoke to able to help you? Did someone have to call you back? If so, how long did it take them to do so? What parts of the experience of dealing with your company impressed you? Which parts could have been handled better? Did you feel that people were doing their best to help, or that you were getting the runaround? Did you feel that that the people you spoke with genuinely wanted to help but were hamstrung by inflexible procedures and systems?

When you find something that could have been done better, the bad news is you have a problem. The good news is that you are now aware of it, and you can think about the best way to improve the way you do things.

Go to your website. How easy is it to find what you want there? Imagine you are someone who is considering doing business with your organisation. What parts of the website impress you? What parts are unclear or unhelpful?

Sometimes websites concentrate too much on showing everyone how clever the company is and not enough on clearly explaining how it can help clients and customers. Putting yourself in the mindset of your customer will help you to focus on what *they* want and how your company can provide it.

Think about how you can improve your customer's experience. For example, some courier companies have introduced an innovation that allows customers to track the location of their parcel online using a consignment number. This benefits the courier company because if people can check the progress of their parcel for themselves, then they don't need to call the company. In addition, knowing that they can easily find out exactly where their parcel is gives customers peace of mind and so improves their experience.

Getting the customer to take one extra step

Before a customer does business with a company, they take a number of steps. For example, before someone buys a product from a company's website they have to:

1 want to find the website

2 find the website

3 look at the home page

4 find the product they want

5 be satisfied that this product meets their needs

6 be satisfied that the price is competitive

7 be satisfied that they can afford it

8 select the item

9 go through the checkout process

10 pay for the item.

Similarly, a number of steps must also be taken before someone engages a plumber, a management consultant or a lawyer. For example, before a client engages lawyer A they:

1 recognise the need to contact a lawyer

2 must be aware that lawyer A exists

3 decide to contact lawyer A

4 (usually) have an initial contact in which they are satisfied that lawyer A might be someone they want to do business with

5 book an appointment with lawyer A

6 decide, after an initial meeting, to continue the relationship

7 reach agreement on fees.

How does a customer or client start to do business with you or your organisation? Break it down into a number of steps. Think like a customer and go through each of those steps. Are any of them tricky, difficult or in any way uncomfortable? If so, you have found an opportunity for innovation.

Think about ways that you might be able to make it easier for a client or customer to take each step.

Here's an example. Ten years ago newspaper headlines were designed to give you the gist of the story. For example, if the government's budget was unpopular, the headline might read 'PM's Horror Budget'.

Now, with so much news consumed online, one of the steps that online news providers want their customers to take is to click through to as many stories as possible so they view more advertising. Whereas headlines used to be informative, now they aim to be intriguing. To write a headline that gets customers to take that extra step and click through to the story, today's headline writer has to be very good at thinking like a customer and working out what combination of five to ten words will most likely entice them to click on the story.

A news.com.au lead story in 2014 showed a head-and-shoulders photo of a young man in his twenties. The headline read:

> **Why we need more like Rhys**
>
> He's in hot demand and without more young people like him we will all feel the squeeze.

I was intrigued. Who was Rhys? Why did we need more people like him? What terrible thing would happen if Rhys, and those like him, stopped doing whatever it is they do? So I clicked.

Rhys, apparently, was a bricklayer and the story was about how Australia was in danger of facing a shortage of bricklayers. I read the first couple of lines and then shut the window. I'm sure a bricklayer shortage is important, but if the headline had been something like 'Australia faces shortage of bricklayers', I would never have clicked through. I'd been manipulated into taking the next step, and I had to admire the cleverness of the headline writer who had found a way to make a story about bricklaying intriguing. He or she had thought like a customer.

Here's another one. A recent story on a news website was headed something like 'The one big secret to losing weight'. I clicked—and discovered that the one big secret to losing weight is to eat less. Not that big a secret, really, but they still got me to click.

So what will make your customer take the next step? What is going to make them decide to commit? Think like a customer to find out. Get right inside their heads, think about what they want, then give it to them.

Ask yourself, 'What am I trying to get customers to do?'

Then ask, 'How can I make it easier for them to do it?'

For example, imagine your customers were in a competitor's store. What would you like them to do? Ideally, you would like them to run out of your competitor's store as fast as they could and straight to your nearest store. Yeah, right! As if that's going to happen!

Innovation does not have to involve a break-out idea, but sometimes it does. This story illustrates what you can achieve when you start asking yourself simple questions about what your customer really wants.

Meat Pack is a shoe store in Guatemala. They sell the big brands, sometimes at a discount, and have lots of young customers. They wanted to come up with a new promotion that was innovative and surprised their customers, so they developed a new feature for their app called 'Hijack'.

When GPS tracking technology recognised that one of their customers was entering a competitor's store, it triggered an opportunity for that customer to earn a discount at a Meat Pack store. The app would flash up '99%', then '98%', then '97%' ... and so on. The quicker the customer got out of the competitor's store and found a Meat Pack store, the bigger the discount they could get. If they got to the Meat Pack store when the app read '65%', they were entitled to a 65 per cent discount. If it took them a bit longer and they arrived when the app read '28%', they were entitled to a 28 per cent discount.

So people would walk into other shoe shops, then pull out their phone and immediately turn around and sprint as fast as they could to the nearest Meat Pack store!

It's a brilliant idea, and very clearly shows that Meat Pack knew how to motivate their customers. What did their customer want? Good shoes at a discount. And if they had to run to get them, they would.

Here's an example of a business *not* bothering to think like a customer.

Someone I know was looking for a new financial adviser. She got a recommendation from someone she trusted and looked at the company's website, which was full of information about how the company helped clients to make good decisions and increase their wealth and financial security. My friend was impressed and went to look for information about the people who ran the company.

She looked all over the site but couldn't find any information about the people who would actually be advising her. There was just an email address and phone number for her to call to get more information. So my friend shut the window and looked elsewhere.

What she wanted was some information about the people who were going to be telling her what she should do with her money. She wanted to read that they were properly qualified and had lots of experience advising people. In short, she wanted to be made to feel safe.

The company had made a mistake. On their website they had concentrated on showing everyone how clever and successful they were. That's good. But if they had put themselves in their client's shoes and thought like a customer, they would have realised that they weren't just selling financial advice — they were selling trust. My friend was not about to trust her life savings, the money that was going to keep her secure and comfortable in her old age, to a *business*. She was going to entrust it to *people*, and she wanted to find out a bit about those people. When she couldn't find that information, she didn't feel safe, so she was out of there.

So ask:

- What are you *really* selling? Trust? Convenience? Peace of mind? Excitement? Think of it from a customer's point of view.

- What do your customers or clients want to find out that will make them feel safe doing business with you?

- What do your customers or clients fear? What will cause them to back off?

Get inside their heads, because then you will realise what you need to offer them to get them to commit.

When something goes wrong it's an opportunity

Recently one of our electronic devices stopped working. I rang the manufacturer and they assured me that someone would call me back in an hour. Someone did call me back, but it was four days later. They had damaged their brand in two ways — firstly, by taking so long to call back and secondly, and more significantly, by making a promise they did not keep. That stuff matters. Customers remember.

Go right through every type of interaction that your organisation has with its customers and clients, and ask:

- Is there any way we could make this better for the customer or client?

- Is there any part of this process that could irritate a customer or client and damage our brand? If so, how can we fix it?

If you supply a good or service to customers or clients, usually your interaction with them is as brief as the customer or client can make it. For example, no one wants to spend more time buying a new phone, vacuum cleaner or car than they need to. They do it as quickly as they can, then they get out of there and hope it is a long time before they have to come back. That's normal. Similarly, people will spend no more time with their accountant, IT consultant, plumber or lawyer than they have to. People just want to get their problem solved as quickly as possible and then get on with their lives.

When something goes wrong, however, the interaction between the customer and the business has to resume. For example, imagine that a customer buys a new computer, then three months later something goes wrong with it and they have to send it back to the manufacturer. Between the time the computer develops a problem and the time the customer gets their computer back, all fixed, they will form a strong impression of the company. If the company acts like it cares, tries to minimise the inconvenience to the customer and treats the customer well, then, even though the company sold the customer a computer that broke, the customer may end up thinking more highly of the company than they would have if the computer had not failed.

If, however, the customer feels like the company doesn't care and shows no sense of urgency in fixing the problem, or the customer feels that they were treated badly, they will probably remember that the next time they buy a new computer.

When thinking like a customer, look at every aspect of what happens when things go wrong for your customers and clients. Then ask how you can improve the process. How can you make your customer feel like they are being cared for and that the company understands the inconvenience the problem has caused? Can you supply a temporary replacement product? Can you ensure that the faulty product is repaired and returned as soon as possible? Can you give the customer a gift voucher by way of apology? Can someone simply ring the customer to apologise personally?

If the impression the customer is left with is, 'Wow! Something went wrong, but they really did everything they could to take care of me', then the customer is likely to come back. If their impression is, 'They did what they had to do under the warranty, but they didn't seem to care about how much hassle it all caused me', then they might not.

CHECKLIST 4: DISCOVERING WHAT YOUR CUSTOMERS WANT

- Experience every aspect of your business *as a customer or client.*

- Ask, 'What do our customers or clients really want? What do they not want?'

- How can you make it easier for a potential customer or client to take the next step?

- Work out what other goods and services your customers or clients might want, and see if you can supply it to them.

- When things go wrong, it's an opportunity to demonstrate to clients and customers that you *care.*

8. Plan for failure

Often when we have carefully put in place thorough and efficient systems, procedures and rules, we convince ourselves that everything will now be all right. But what if something goes wrong? Have you planned for failure? If something goes wrong, will the result be a minor inconvenience, or a major disaster?

A lot of people wonder why aeroplanes still have ashtrays in the toilets, given that smoking has been outlawed for years. Are they just really old planes? Has the airline not bothered to remove them? The reason the ashtrays are there is in case the airline's systems don't work and someone breaks the rules. If a passenger decides that, despite the clear prohibition, they just *have* to smoke a cigarette, where are they going to do it? Probably in the toilet. How are they going to get rid of the (possibly still smouldering) butt? They might try to flush it down the toilet or they might put it in the waste bin, which might be full of used paper towels. That could start a fire, which, in a plane high in the sky, would be bad. The airline provides an ashtray in the toilet so if anyone *does* flout the ban on smoking, they at least have somewhere safe to dispose of the butt.

The airlines haven't presumed that their rule will always be followed. Instead, they have been smart enough to assume that it will occasionally be broken, and asked this: when the rule *is* broken, what can we do to make sure that nothing really bad happens?

I try to avoid putting a glass of water on the same surface as my computer. I'm not especially clumsy. I can't remember the last time I knocked over a cup or a glass. But if I *do* knock one over, I don't want it to ruin my computer. By ensuring the glass and the computer aren't on the same surface, I'm planning for failure. When I do knock over a glass, it's not going to be a disaster.

Look at your own rules and ask: when they *are* broken, what are the consequences? When the breaking of a rule could have an unpleasant or harmful result, see if you can plan for failure and do something that will minimise those consequences.

Pull all your systems and processes apart, and work out what will happen if each part of a process or system fails. Where you identify significant potential consequences, plan for failure and think about what you can do to minimise them.

CHECKLIST 5: BREAKING OUT OF HABITUAL THINKING

- ☐ Question everything.

- ☐ Identify all the assumptions you are making. Are you sure they are all valid?

- ☐ Technology is not always the answer (but sometimes it is).

- ☐ Reframe the question. If you can't get *everything* you want, is there a way of being a bit less ambitious and still getting *most* of what you want?

- ☐ Sometimes the solution is right in front of our eyes. Is the answer in your data?

- ☐ Think like a customer or client.

- ☐ Plan for failure. If something goes wrong, how can you ensure that the result is merely inconvenience and not disaster?

Four reasons why we don't think enough

I hope that by now you have been persuaded, if you needed to be, that thinking about how to make things better is a useful, productive and necessary part of every business. Why, then, don't we do more of it?

When I speak to audiences about innovation, I often ask them why they think we don't spend more time thinking about how to make things better. These are the most common responses.

'I don't have time'

This is the most common reason people give for not spending more time thinking about how to improve their business, and it's perfectly understandable. People aren't joking when they say they're busy. But if you spend *all* your time on today's problems, and *none* of it on getting ready for tomorrow, I suggest you need to adjust your priorities. Things are going to change. They always have done. If you don't work out how to make your business better, in five years' time it may have slipped backwards.

So how do you find the time? It's all about attitude and priorities.

The reason why people say they are too busy to think about ways to do things better is because at some level, conscious or unconscious, they don't see innovation as being as important as the rest of their work. They see it as something extra, something that you do once all the real work is done.

If you think something is important, then you make time for it. Have you ever heard someone say this? 'I did all the work getting the customer interested, overcoming their objections and getting them ready to commit, but once I had done all that I was out of time, so I didn't actually sell them the car, even though they were really keen. Hopefully they'll come back tomorrow and I can do it then.' No one would ever say that, of course, because everyone knows that making sales is vital to any business.

Unfortunately innovation is easy work to put off. Thinking about ways to make things better doesn't feel as urgent as closing a deal. But coming up with an innovative idea can be far more valuable to your business than closing one deal or making one sale.

When you feel like putting innovation off, remind yourself that everything is going to be different ten years from now, and that your business is either going to be making the changes or getting left behind by them.

If you think innovation is important, find time to work on it. I'm not talking about devoting half your life to innovation — just 1 or 2 per cent of your work time. Schedule ten minutes a day for thinking about how to improve what you do. It's not much. Put it in your diary. Do it at the same time each day, and make sure you don't take on any other commitments at that time. When your thinking time comes around, turn your phone off. Maybe it will work better for you if you get out of your normal workspace.

It's hard to *create* a habit, but it's not hard to *keep* a habit. I do twenty minutes of yoga every morning. It's not hard to make myself do it, because it's a habit. I've been doing it for two and a half years, so now I don't even think about *not* doing it. But *creating* the habit was really hard. I needed to be really determined. I didn't like doing the exercises. They hurt. A lot. But I just made myself, and then after about a month it stopped being an incredibly hard thing that I had to make myself do, and simply became a habit. Now it's just what I do when I wake up. I don't even think about whether or not I *want* to do it. I just do it, like cleaning my teeth.

The good thing about creating a habit is that you don't have to have a battle every day about whether or not to make the effort. Negotiating with yourself can be really energy consuming and time wasting. You spend all this time arguing with yourself, and by the time you finish the argument you could have been half finished.

If you want to spend more time being innovative, take the negotiating out of it and just make one simple rule: that you will spend ten minutes a day trying to think of ways of doing things better. That way you don't need willpower. You just need to follow the rule.

That's how I wrote my first novel for children. I realised that after we put the kids to bed I used to watch television for an hour or so, and that I could use that time for writing. So I made one simple rule: I would not watch television until I had finished working on my novel. Every night, instead of watching TV, I wrote. I didn't have to agonise over whether I was going to write, or when I was going to write. I just made it real simple. After the kids went to bed, instead of watching TV, I wrote for an hour.

If you have the *motivation* to spend more time trying to be innovative, that's great, but you're only halfway there. You also need the *determination* to create a habit. Starting the habit will be hard, but once you embed it, *keeping* the habit will be much easier.

'I'm just not creative'

People often make this claim to rationalise why they don't spend more time thinking about better ways of doing things. Here's my response: *Yes, you are!* When you were a kid you used to paint and draw and make up games and pretend to be other people and other creatures *all day long*. That was your job! You really want to try to tell me that none of that was creative! If you were creative as a kid, then you can be creative as an adult. Maybe you haven't been *exercising* your creativity as much lately as you used to, but that doesn't mean it's gone away. Your biceps don't go away if you don't exercise them. They're still there, and when you start exercising them again, they grow.

I blame the advertising industry. It perpetuates the myth that some people are creative and others aren't by labelling those who do a particular job 'creatives'. The implication is that everyone else isn't.

I have met hundreds of people who have come up with fantastic inventions, great innovations and smart ways of doing things better, and many of them were people you wouldn't necessarily immediately identify as creative. Some were quiet, shy, logical people; some probably wouldn't do great in an IQ test; and many do jobs you wouldn't necessarily associate with creativity.

Labelling yourself as 'not creative' can be a cop-out. Deciding that you are not creative is your escape clause. You don't have to go through the difficult process of staring at a blank piece of paper and trying to fill it with new ideas, because you've already decided you are incapable of coming up with anything original.

Often when people say they are not creative, what they really mean is that they lack confidence. Even when they *do* think of an idea, as soon as they hit an obstacle—and there will *always* be obstacles—they feel as if they have just discovered proof that they are incapable and give up.

Stop worrying about whether or not you are 'creative'. It's not the most important factor in being innovative. The most important factor is determination. I've said before that innovators aren't inherently different from the rest of us, but there is one thing they usually do better than most others. They will wrestle with a problem relentlessly, without giving up, for much longer than the rest of us. When a problem gets difficult and we don't feel like we are getting anywhere, most of us stop. Innovators keep going. They are determined enough to keep failing for longer than the rest of us. And in doing so, sometimes they succeed.

Creativity is overrated. Determination and perseverance are underrated.

When I'm writing a novel I don't wait for 'creative inspiration'. I look at a blank page and start writing down the first idea I can think of that seems like it might be half decent. Usually it's not very good, so then I work really hard to make it better. If I sat around waiting for the perfect idea, I'd never get anywhere. Everything good I've written has started out being not very good. Then I rewrite it and rewrite it, aiming to make it better each time.

In the innovation workshops I run, I ask people to identify opportunities for innovation in their business and then to think of ways of taking advantage of those opportunities. As far as I am aware, in all those workshops no one has ever—*ever*—been unable to come up with at least one idea to improve the way that they do things. Hundreds and hundreds of very different people—nurses, event organisers, schoolkids, managers, bankers—and they have all been able to think of some sort of innovative idea to improve what they do. And I only give them about six minutes to do it!

Don't worry about whether you are more or less creative than other people. Just look for opportunities for innovation, and then wrestle with them until you have something. If you don't think that what you come up is very good, that's okay. See if you can make it better.

'Innovation isn't part of my job'

Another reason people give for not spending more time thinking of ways to improve what they do is they think that innovation is not part of their job. Yes, it is. Whatever your job is, coming up with ways to do it better should be a part of it.

I understand that many organisations think the job of the person who, for example, makes widgets is just to make widgets. But smart organisations recognise that they need to be continually improving the way they make those widgets, and they make it clear that everyone in the organisation should be trying to think of how to do just that.

Of course, many organisations don't do this. I'll discuss this in more detail in chapter 7, but for the moment let me emphasise that innovation *should* be part of everyone's job. Everyone should always be trying to think of better ways of doing things.

The previous three justifications are commonly given by people for not thinking more about how to do things better. However, I think the biggest reason people don't think more is this:

'Thinking is hard!'

No argument here. Thinking *is* hard. It really is. If you take my advice and identify some opportunities for innovation in your business and then write one of them at the top of a blank page and start thinking about it, what comes next?

You find yourself staring at a blank piece of paper, and if a great idea doesn't pop immediately into your head, you probably start to feel frustrated and stupid. Before too long you'll probably find yourself thinking, 'This is too hard. I can't do it'.

Here's the thing. If that's what's happening, then it means you're doing it right.

Thinking is hard. It just is. It's hard for everyone.

The terrifying blank page

When I'm writing a children's novel, at some point I get up to page 165. I think to myself, 'That's pretty good'. Then I turn to page 166 and it's blank, and usually I have no idea how I am going to fill it. Before too long I start to feel stupid and frustrated. The good news is that it's normal to feel this way. I've interviewed many authors, including some very famous and big-selling ones, and I usually ask them if they still find writing hard. Almost all of them say they do.

These days, most mornings we're confronted by a checklist of about thirty-eight things that we have to do. It's not often that we find ourselves staring at a blank page, and when we do, it can be intimidating.

Innovation requires us to think of something new. In most jobs, most of the time we do variations on tasks that we have done many times before. Usually we are reacting to things and generally it's easier to *react* than to *act*, because the parameters of what you have to do have already been set. For example, if your boss sends you an email asking you to do three things, you react by doing them. Of course, that's not always easy, but it's more structured than staring at a blank page and trying to think of a new idea. When we challenge ourselves to spend time trying to think of new ways to improve our business, it can feel uncomfortable, unfamiliar and daunting. Sometimes, because it feels that way, we leap to the conclusion that we mustn't be any good at it. Don't!

Innovation is hard! It's a lot harder than answering an email. It's supposed to be. Try not to be intimidated by the blank page. Believe it or not, there have been many times in your life when you have been confronted by a blank page, and you have filled it.

At school you would have been faced with many blank pages that you filled with stories and ideas and essays. Perhaps when you finished school your future was a blank page, and you had to work out for yourself what you wanted to do. Probably there have been other times when the course ahead has been unclear, but nonetheless you have worked your way through it.

Think about the organisation you work for. It may have begun with someone who didn't know what to do next, who thought hard and eventually decided to do something new and start the business you now work in.

Your favourite book, your favourite film, your favourite piece of music—they all came from someone staring at a blank page and wondering how they were going to fill it. The great thing about a blank page is that there is no formula, no status quo, no assumptions, no 'right' way of doing things. There is just you and your thoughts. Some very good things come from filling blank pages.

Most of us work in jobs in which we follow a process or method to accomplish most of our tasks. Some industries, however, have in-built blank pages. Advertising, for example. They have process and systems, but they also have to keep thinking up new ideas. A client might say, 'We want a thirty-second ad for our new chocolate bar. Show us what you've got in two weeks'.

So in advertising they are forced to be innovative. They have to stare at a blank thirty-second spot, and work out an intriguing, informative and entertaining way to fill it. Innovation is an essential part of their job.

Release the pressure

One reason why some people never fill those blank pages is they put too much pressure on themselves to come up with a *great* idea right away. Don't hold out for a great idea. Just aim for *some sort of an idea*. You can worry about whether it's great or not later. The important thing is just to get something down. Getting something down is useful for a few reasons:

1 It builds confidence. Once you have proved to yourself that you are capable of having a new idea, then next time it might be a bit easier.

2 Sometimes an idea that initially doesn't look very good grows to become something of value.

3 Coming up with any kind of idea is good practice. Even if that idea doesn't end up going anywhere, just going through the process is useful. Most innovators failed before they succeeded, and from each idea that didn't blossom they learned something. The more you practise exercising the innovative part of your mind, the better.

Challenge yourself, or your team, with a blank page. Pick a problem or an opportunity, write it at the top of a blank page, and think. If you get distracted or bored, that's okay. Just pull yourself back to the task at hand. Don't worry about having *good* ideas. Just have ideas.

Get bored

If you are trying to be innovative and you can't think of any ideas, you might start to feel bored. That's when some people stop. Keep going! If you do, your boredom might even help you to come up with an idea.

In 2014 Dr Sandi Mann and Rebekah Cadman from the School of Psychology at the University of East Lancashire did some experiments to try to learn more about the relationship between boredom and creativity. They asked forty people to come up with different ways they could use two polystyrene cups, a task that required some creativity. Then they asked forty different people to complete the same task, but before this second group did so, they had them copy phone numbers out of the phone book for fifteen minutes, a deliberately boring task.

The second group, who had done something boring first, came up with more creative responses than the first group.

They did a second experiment with three groups of thirty people. Group 1 did just the creative task. Group 2 copied out phone numbers and then did the creative task. Group 3 had to do something even more passive and boring: before they did the creative task they had to *read* a list of phone numbers.

The researchers found that, again, the people in Group 1 were the least creative. They also found that those in Group 3 who had just *read* the names were more creative than those in Group 2 who had to *write* them out. The conclusion they drew was that a more passive boring activity like reading can stimulate more creativity. Dr Mann said, 'Boredom at work has always been seen as something to be eliminated, but perhaps we should be embracing it in order to enhance our creativity'.

If you start trying to think of an idea and get bored, don't worry. Firstly, it's normal. Secondly, if you persist then the period of boredom may well be followed by a period of enhanced creativity.

CHECKLIST 6: OVERCOMING EXCUSES TO AVOID THINKING

- ◻ *'I don't have time.'* Find ten minutes a day and book it in your diary.

- ◻ *'I'm just not creative.'* Yes, you are! You're not incapable of being creative. Maybe you're just out of practice.

- ◻ *'Innovation isn't part of my job.'* Well, it should be.

- ◻ *Thinking is hard.'* Too right it is, but it's worthwhile.

What if you're stuck?

It's not unusual to get stuck when trying to think of new ideas. Imagine how many times the inventors of the telephone or the car or the electric light or peanut butter got stuck. It's a normal part of the process, so try not to beat yourself up. Here are some strategies that might help when you get stuck.

Break out of habitual thinking

Go through the strategies outlined earlier in this chapter to help you to break out of habitual ways of thinking.

◻ Question everything you do. Could there be a better way?

◻ What assumptions are you making?

◻ Maybe technology is not the answer (or maybe it is).

◻ Are some insights available from analysing your data?

◻ Would it help to think like a customer or a client?

Here are some other strategies.

Load up with information

If you are trying to think of ways to improve the efficiency of your supply chain, then find out as much as you can about it. Read everything you can find, talk to people who know more about it than you do, and find out how other organisations run their supply chain.

The more you know about an area, the more likely you are to be able to come up with some ideas to improve it. In addition, the time you spend collecting information about the area you are trying to improve is time that your mind is thinking about it, and the more time you spend thinking about it, the more likely you are to come up with an idea to make it better.

Give your mind some time and space—disconnect!

Earlier I talked about how smartphones and connectedness, while useful in many ways, have reduced the frequency of quiet moments we used to get throughout the day in which to think. Ideas often come when we least expect them, when our minds are disengaged and free to wander and make connections between seemingly unrelated things. If you are stuck, find some time each day to disconnect electronically, turn off and daydream. Maybe while you are on the bus or walking home, or at lunchtime. If your mind is always cluttered and busy, it's hard for a new idea to find room to grow.

Exercise

Get outside and go for a walk or a run. Whenever I go for a walk or run I always have a least one idea. It's not always a great idea, but it's usually something that helps a bit. It may be for a book I am writing or a speech I have to give. Take something with you to record any ideas that occur to you. I take my phone when I run, and then leave a voice message. The only problem is that when I get home and play it back, usually all I hear is panting!

If you exercise in a gym where there are televisions on, or you always have headphones on and music playing, give yourself some quiet time. Don't crowd thoughts out.

Often the payoff comes later

When I started doing stand-up comedy, I was working full-time as a lawyer. Every Saturday afternoon I sat at my desk and tried to write jokes. It wasn't much fun. Jokes are really hard to write and often at the end of two or three hours I'd have nothing usable. Sometimes I would spend ages wrestling with a concept that I thought was funny but be unable to find the right way of turning it into a joke that an audience would laugh at. I would think I had wasted my time but then, often, sometime in the next day or two, I would see or hear something that would show me a fresh way of looking at it, and suddenly the way to tell the joke would be obvious.

Coming up with innovative ideas can be like that. You might not get an idea during the ten minutes you devote to trying to think of one, but the more time you spend trying to think of ideas, the more likely it is that one will come.

Just let the problem or opportunity sit, keep it in your mind, and something might come to you on the bus home, or in the shower, or while you are walking to work. You might hear someone say something, or read or see something, that triggers a connection.

Stay with it, and keep open

When I do public speaking workshops and I talk about humour, I tell people that the most important thing is to be open and on the lookout for it. It's the same with ideas. Be patient. Stay open, keep the problem and opportunity in your mind, and something might come to you at the most unexpected time.

Sleep with a pen and paper by your bed in case you think of something before you go to sleep. If you wake up in the middle of the night with an idea, write it down, but make sure you make it legible. I once woke up in the middle of the night with a perfectly formed joke in my brain. Without turning on the light, I wrote it down on my pad. Next morning, no matter how hard I tried to decipher it, it was just scribble. I think one of the words might have been *banana*. Or maybe *bandana*. I still think about that joke. I know it was brilliant.

While I was writing this book it was always in my mind, and as a result I was constantly open to seeing new examples of innovation, or seeing how incidents in my own life were relevant to the topic I was writing about.

Talk to someone

Sometimes sharing a problem, an opportunity or a half-formed idea with someone else can open doors. Maybe the other person can help to advance your idea or solve your problem, but even if they can't, the process of sharing it might help you to clarify your own thoughts. As you discuss the problem with someone, something new might occur to you, or a question that the other person asks, or a comment they make, might spark something.

Once you have an idea, expand it

Once you have an idea, try not to think about all the reasons why it might not work. Just focus on growing it. Brainstorm. Write down as many thoughts as you can about your idea without stopping to judge them.

Ideas often come from soft, dreamy, creative and imaginative thinking. It's important not to get too bogged down in detail too early. Just let the idea come and try to grow it in whatever direction it goes.

Soft mind, hard mind

Once you have done that, it's time to get a bit more hard-headed. We need a soft, dreamy mind to come up with ideas, but then to iron out all their problems and to start getting our ideas closer to becoming a reality, we have to get a bit more hard-headed and strategic and focus on the details. Engage with all the practical problems that your idea presents, and try to solve them.

Then actively look for *more* problems. It is better that you find them now, rather than someone else finding them later. Share your idea with others and ask them what problems and opportunities they see. If someone points out a problem that you hadn't thought of, try not to get defensive. Instead, look for solutions.

Try to work out how much time and money it's going to take to develop your idea. How much will it cost to trial it? How much to implement it?

Then try to work out how much money the idea could make or save. Don't do any of this on gut feel alone. Do the sums. There's no point spending a lot of time and money developing an idea that isn't going to save as much money as it costs to implement. The idea might be brilliant, elegant and revolutionary, but if it's not going to help the bottom line, then it's probably time to set it down and move on to the next one.

If you think your idea might be viable, then work out the mechanics of its implementation. Go through all the stages of your idea, from start to finish:

- How will the idea work? Have you got everything covered, or are there some gaps? If there are, can you figure out how to fill them, or do you need some help? If so, who might be able to help?

- List all the problems your idea might have, and then think about how you might be able to overcome them.

- If you get stuck on a problem, share it with others and see if they can offer a different perspective that helps.

- If you are still stuck, step back and assess the problem. Is the problem fatal to the idea or just a minor detail? If you cannot solve the problem, will the idea still have value?

- What is the next thing you need to do to grow your idea? (More on this in chapter 3.) How much will taking that step cost? What are the potential benefits of taking that next step? What other steps will need to be taken to make your idea a reality?

- If your idea is implemented, what will it mean for the people in your organisation? Who will implement the idea? Will the idea's implementation change anyone's job? If so, what does it mean for those affected?

- What will your idea cost to implement? Try to cost it, in time and money, as best you can. What will it cost to run?

- What will be the benefits of implementing the idea? Again, try to arrive at a reasonably accurate estimate of how much money implementing the idea will make or save. If you can show that your idea is going to make or save more money than it costs, it's going to be a powerful argument in favour of its implementation.

- Who do you need to convince to advance the idea? Anticipate all the objections that others may have, and work out what your response to them will be.

CHECKLIST 7:
GETTING UNSTUCK

If you are trying to solve a problem, or take advantage of an opportunity for innovation, and you get stuck:

- Find out as much information about the area as you can.

- Don't fill every spare moment with your smartphone. Give yourself time and space to think and daydream.

- Discuss the problem or opportunity with someone else

- Exercise.

- Be patient.

Once you have an idea:

- Grow it in as many directions as you can without stopping to judge.

- Then get practical. Anticipate all the problems your idea might have, and try to solve them.

Chapter 2

VALUE

The first step in innovation is to have an idea. The second is to *value* your idea. That is, to treat it like it is important. That sounds simple but it's not, because when we have an idea we don't necessarily know whether it's brilliant, ridiculously stupid or somewhere in between. The temptation is often to think it's no good and to let it go.

When an idea comes, there's usually an initial surge of excitement, but soon the doubts set in:

- 'It's probably no good.'

- 'There must be a problem with it that I haven't seen yet.'

- 'What if it doesn't work?'

- 'How could *I* think of a great idea?'

- 'Surely if it was a good idea, someone else would have already thought of it.'

It's normal to doubt the quality of your idea. Do you think those who first thought of the wheel or frozen yoghurt or the scarf *knew* immediately they were onto a winner? They probably experienced the same doubts as you and I do, and the same mixture of excitement and uncertainty.

Over the years many people have approached me and said, 'You know that thing you had on *The New Inventors...* I thought of that *years* ago'.

I always say, 'Great! Well done!', because thinking of a better way of doing things is always worthy of congratulation. Then I ask, 'And what did you do when you had the idea?'

And often they will pause, look at the ground and say, 'Nothing'.

Their idea had never gone beyond being just that—an idea. They had never discovered how good it could get, because they hadn't valued it highly enough to find out.

An idea that remains locked in your mind and is never let out into the world can't change anything. The only way to find out if an idea is any good is to value it, and grow it.

Imagine how you would feel if you thought of an idea, but because you doubted its value you didn't do anything with it, and then later someone else had the same idea, developed it and made a success of it.

Don't let it happen!

One reason we can be reluctant to value our ideas is that we fear failure. What if we have an idea and it doesn't work? We might look and feel stupid.

We have all met people who constantly tell their colleagues all the things management *should* be doing, but who never actually share their own ideas. By keeping their ideas from those who might be able to assess and implement them, they protect themselves from being judged, and from the possibility of discovering that their ideas aren't quite as good as they think they are.

If you want to innovate, it's important that you develop a healthy relationship with failure, because it is an inevitable part of the process of innovation. It is very rare to succeed without first failing. Think of something you are good at: your job, playing piano, push-ups, sailing, reading, whatever ... Were you good at it the first time you did it? In all probability you weren't. Who sits down at the piano for the first time and plays well? Who tries reading for the first time and completely nails it?

The way to get good at something is to try, fail, try again, fail again, try some more ... and slowly get better. It's the same with having new ideas. I don't know of any innovator who claims that every idea they have ever had has been successful. Innovators often have to go through many ideas to get to the one that works.

As educator Ken Robinson puts it, 'If you're not prepared to be wrong, you'll never come up with anything original'. Innovators do not fear failure; they embrace it. 'Failure should be our teacher, not our undertaker,' writes Denis Waitley. 'Failure is delay, not defeat. It is a temporary detour, not a dead end. Failure is something we can avoid only by saying nothing, doing nothing, and being nothing.'

Others have captured the same idea in different ways:

'Only those who dare to fail greatly can ever achieve greatly.'

Robert F. Kennedy

'I have not failed. I've just found 10 000 ways that won't work.'

Thomas Edison

Accept that failure is part of the process. Try to take the pressure off yourself to have a *great* idea and, instead, accept that having *any* idea is a good start. Value every idea that you have. Ideas are our point of difference as a species. They have taken us out of the cave and allowed us to create the sophisticated and ingenious world we live in. Treat every one like it is important.

Innovators want to find out how good every idea they have is. And when they discover that one is not so good, that's okay. They learn what they can from their failure and move on, and try to think of another idea. Only a small percentage of ideas will grow into things you can implement in your business, but it's very hard to get to the good ones without going through all of them.

Ideas are like balloons

It's really easy to punch holes in a half-formed idea, be it your own or someone else's. When the inventor of the wheel or the telephone or the wheelbarrow or the toothbrush or the jam-filled doughnut first had their idea, it wouldn't have been difficult to find fault with it.

Try to resist the temptation to engage your inner critic too early and to judge ideas before you give them a chance to grow. Of course we have to judge our ideas at some point, but let the idea get as good as it can get first. Very few ideas sound great when they are first thought of. Sometimes we can be so judgmental of ourselves (and others) that as soon as we have an idea we start to look for all the things that are wrong with it. Often we are trained to look for problems, and our first instinct when confronted with a new idea is to poke holes in it. It's not hard to find fault with a new idea. The wheel, for example:

- 'Surely it will just fall over.'

- 'It will be too hard to make them perfectly round.'

- 'Even if you can get it to roll along, how can you carry anything on it?'

- 'If you make it out of stone it will be too heavy, but if you make it out of wood it won't be strong enough.'

- 'I just don't think there's a market for it. People are used to carrying things themselves.'

When you have an idea, try to suspend judgement for a while and just ask one simple question:

'How can I make it better?'

Treat ideas like balloons. Blow them up as big as they can get before you judge them. If you showed an empty balloon to someone who had never seen one before, they would think it was just a shrivelled up piece of plastic. Once you blow it up, though, it becomes a lot more impressive.

When you have an idea, brainstorm it enthusiastically. Grow it without stopping to criticise or to think about whether the things you are thinking of are good or bad. Don't stand in judgement—just think. The aim is to grow the idea as much as you can, in as many different directions as you can, and to discover how big the idea can get. Judgement can come later.

At high school, one of my English teachers would come into the room and say, 'Write! Write! Write!' We would start to ask him what he wanted us to write about, but he would cut us off. 'Just write. Write for five minutes. Don't stop. Write anything. Just write.'

It was a great lesson in not judging ourselves too early. Instead of agonising over whether a sentence was completely perfect, before we knew it we had written a page without any interference from our inner critic. Once the words were down on paper, we could go back, judge them and work out how to make what we had written better.

Hold the phone

Have you ever experienced this? You have an idea, then the phone rings. You answer and afterwards you go to write down your idea ... and it's gone! And it *never* comes back.

Ideas can arrive at odd times, and so can phone calls. When you have an idea, *drop everything* and write it down. If the phone rings, ignore it. If your spouse calls you, ignore that too. If you are walking along the beach and someone is drowning, and you have an idea, ig—...no, wait! Some things are more important than ideas. But not many.

Treat ideas like they are important. When you have one, make a note of it straight away. Keep thinking about the idea and developing it.

Listen sometimes, don't listen sometimes

As you begin to share your idea with others, you will get feedback and comments. Sometimes you should listen to them and sometimes you shouldn't. The hard bit is to work out when to do what.

Here's the thing. When it comes to innovation, no one knows what's going to work. A lot of people *think* they know, and have intelligent-sounding arguments that back up their point of view, but no one actually *knows*.

Keep open to advice, and listen to those who urge you to be cautious. It is foolhardy to ignore well-intentioned counsel. Keep in mind, though, that there have been many instances in the past when people who have had a great deal of expertise have confidently written off innovations and inventions—and got it way wrong!

> 'Drill for oil? You mean drill into the ground to try and find oil? You're crazy.'
>
> *Drillers who Edwin L. Drake tried to enlist for his drilling project in 1859*

> 'This "telephone" has too many shortcomings to be seriously considered as a means of communication. The device is inherently of no value to us.'
>
> *Western Union internal memo, 1876*

'Heavier-than-air flying machines are impossible.'

> *Lord Kelvin, President of the Royal Society, 1895*

'Everything that can be invented has been invented.'

> *Charles H. Duell, Commissioner of the United States Patent and Trademark Office, 1899*

'Who the hell wants to hear actors talk?'

> *H. M. Warner, Warner Brothers, 1927*

'Airplanes are interesting toys but of no military value.'

> *Marshal Ferdinand Foch, Professor of Strategy, École Supérieure de guerre, 1911*

Be mindful of the problems and the obstacles that need to be overcome to turn your idea into reality; be realistic about the risks that are involved; and be open to the possibility of failure.

To be an innovator you need perseverance and determination. Of course, there is sometimes a fine line between determination and obsession, and it's important not to get too blinkered, and to be clear-headed in assessing the progress of your idea. Some innovators find it difficult to let go of an idea they are attached to, even when everyone else has concluded that it will never work. Occasionally they confound everyone and make their idea work in spite of the doubters. Other times they spend all their money and end up frustrated and broke.

Accept that there will be obstacles, work hard to overcome them, but try to remain objective. If you think you have become too close to your idea and may have lost that objectivity, then ask someone you trust for their opinion on whether the idea has run its course. Remember, if one idea doesn't work, there's always another one.

CHECKLIST 8:
VALUING YOUR IDEA

- When you have an idea, self-doubt is normal.

- Accept that failure is part of the process of innovation.

- Every great idea started out sounding like a stupid idea.

- Before you judge your idea, grow it as big as it can be.

- When an idea comes, drop everything and listen to it.

- There will always be people who doubt your idea. Listen to what they say, but make your own judgements.

Chapter 3

USE

The next thing innovators do better than everyone else is that they *use* their ideas. They do something with them. The cleverest idea in the world won't be worth anything if it remains in the space between our ears. Innovation requires us to act.

However, taking your idea out of your mind and into the real world can be daunting. There are problems to solve, obstacles to overcome, managers to convince, bureaucratic inertia to defeat, and perhaps money to find. All of that takes time and energy, and aren't you busy enough already?

And what if you go to all that effort only to discover that your idea doesn't work! Or that it will cost too much? Or you will have to fight so many battles along the way, and make so many compromises, that it will cause you more pain than it's worth?

These are all, unfortunately, legitimate concerns.

Everyone who has had an innovative idea has faced some, if not all, of these obstacles. But if they hadn't pressed on regardless, then we wouldn't have toasters or flowerpots or tyres. There's only one way to find out how good an idea is, and that is to test it out in the real world.

Do the next thing

Once you have had an idea, and have grown it, it's time to start using it. Here's a way to make using your idea seem more manageable. Don't think about the eighty-six things you need to do to turn your idea into a reality. Just think about the *next* thing. Work out the next thing you need to do to develop your idea. It might be:

◻ writing it down

◻ drawing it

◻ making a flow chart that shows how it works

◻ collaborating with someone who has knowledge or skills you don't possess to get more information

◻ pitching it to someone

◻ designing it

◻ making it

◻ setting up a trial

◻ implementing the idea.

Or it might be something else.

Whatever the next thing to do is, just do that. Don't think about *everything* that needs to be done, just the next thing. Chinese philosopher Lao Tzu said, 'The journey of a thousand miles begins with a single step'. We can all take that single step. And then another one.

Once you work out what the next thing to do is, give yourself a deadline to do it by, and then do it.

Then do that next thing.

Find the end point of each idea

Again, take the pressure off. When developing ideas, your aim shouldn't be to incorporate each one of them into the business. That would be nice, but it's probably not realistic. The aim should be to find the end point of every idea. That is, to make each idea as good as it can be. And if you do that and along the way it becomes clear that the idea isn't good enough to become part of your business, then let it go. We know that only a small percentage of ideas will go all the way to implementation, so the aim should be to find how far each idea can go, as quickly and as cheaply as possible.

Accept that most of the ideas you have, for one reason or another, won't end up being used. That's okay. It's normal. If one in ten, or even one out of twenty, of your ideas is incorporated into what you do and makes a measurable and consistent improvement to your business, then it will probably have been time well spent.

How, then, do you find that one good idea in ten? The only way to get to the one usable idea is to go through *every* idea. We need to advance each and every idea up to the point where it becomes clear that it is not going to improve the way we do things. Don't dismiss an idea until you're *sure* it won't work. Try to avoid acting on hunches. Often hunches are right, but sometimes they're wrong.

The tricky part is to advance your ideas without using up too much time and money. So take small steps. If we accept that most of the ideas we have will fail, then the aim becomes to find the ones that will fail as quickly and cheaply as possible, before we spend too much time and money on them.

If you have ten ideas, don't pick the one you *think* is going to work. Have a process. Move each idea one step forward as cheaply as possible. For each idea work out what the next thing to do is, then do it.

Do it on a small scale, and use the resources you have as cleverly and efficiently as you can. If you don't have sufficient resources to advance every idea, then evaluate the following three factors:

- the potential benefits of the idea
- the likelihood of it becoming a viable part of your business
- the cost of developing the idea.

Then pick the ideas that appear to have the greatest chance of providing a benefit, and advance them.

Move each idea one step forward, then assess the results. It may well be that in taking an idea one step forward, it becomes clear that it isn't going to work, or that it is going to be too expensive to implement, or that it won't produce the benefits you were hoping for, or there are some problems that need to be ironed out before it can progress further.

If that happens, you can either discard that idea, or set it aside for further development. Then the remaining ideas can be taken another step forward. Again, assess the results to see if they indicate that there are any more ideas not worth taking further. In this way, slowly we whittle our ideas down to the most viable ones.

For example, imagine that you have an idea to improve the efficiency of one of your processes. In developing the idea you might discover that while the new process looks more efficient than the old one, the cost of implementing it will be greater than the money it would save. If you grapple with that problem for a while and can't find a solution, then it's time to set that idea aside and move on to the next one.

Don't keep throwing resources at an idea just because you really *like* it, if it's clear that there is a significant problem. Go back and think about how to solve the problem first. Try not to get too attached to your ideas, or to let emotion cloud your judgement. Perhaps you really like an idea and you spent a lot of time developing it. You were excited when you first thought of it and you desperately want it to work. These are *not* good reasons to keep throwing resources at an idea whose end point you have already found.

Failure is part of the innovation process, and every idea that fails gets you closer to the one that will succeed. The only good reason to invest time and money into developing an idea for your business is that you think there is a good chance it could make your business better. So when it becomes clear that an idea *isn't* going to end up being implemented in your business, say goodbye to it.

If your idea fails, it doesn't mean you are stupid or worthless or incapable of being innovative. It just means that that particular idea didn't work. Don't take it personally. It's just an idea.

Operate on as small a scale as possible. If you are doing a trial of an idea in a medium or big business, don't trial it *everywhere*. Just pick one small part of the business to run a trial in. Keep it simple, keep it cheap and don't be scared to say goodbye to ideas that fall over. Every time an idea doesn't work you can think, 'Great! Now I'm one idea closer to the good one'.

Bring in other people

As the idea develops, bring in other minds. At every stage, ask people to look at the idea and give you their opinion on it. Ask:

- What do they think of the idea?

- What do they see as its potential benefits?

- What problems do they see?

- How would they overcome those problems?

- Do they have any suggestions on how to improve the idea?

Talking to other people about your idea is a cheap and effective way of developing it. The hardest part of developing an idea is the start, because you are trying to create something out of nothing. Once you have an idea, then other minds that work a little differently from yours may be able to see opportunities to develop it that you might not have thought of. Or they may spot a problem that you hadn't thought of, and maybe even come up with a way to overcome it.

When developing an idea, whenever you get stuck, talk it over with someone else. Even if they can't solve your problem, it may be that sharing your idea with someone sparks your brain to think in a different way, suggesting a way forward.

Sometimes you need to persist

Sometimes a good idea will require a great deal of persistence to get right.

The all-purpose lubricant WD-40 is used, among other things, to stop tools rusting and hinges squeaking. It's a very successful product. According to surveys by the manufacturer it can be found in up to 80 per cent of American homes and it enjoys sales worth hundreds of millions of dollars each year.

The reason it's called WD-40 is that they had 40 goes at it before they got it right.

You would imagine that after WD-26 had problems they would have been getting pretty fed up, and when they still hadn't nailed it with WD-37 no one would have blamed them if they had thrown in the towel. But they must have known they were onto something, and it was just a matter of continuing to get it wrong and persisting until eventually they got it right.

CHECKLIST 9: DEVELOPING YOUR IDEA

- ◻ When developing your idea, don't get overwhelmed. Just work out the next thing you need to do to grow your idea, and then do it. Then repeat the process.

- ◻ Accept that most ideas won't end up being incorporated into your business. The aim is just to find the end point of every idea.

- ◻ Trial new ideas on a small scale.

- ◻ Fail quickly and cheaply.

- ◻ Keep talking to people about your idea. Get their advice and perspective.

- ◻ Sometimes you need to be persistent.

Chapter 4

HOW TO PITCH AN IDEA

If you have an idea that you want to grow, then sooner or later you are probably going to have to pitch it to someone. In fact, to grow your idea and turn it into something real, you may need to pitch it dozens of times. Inside an organisation, you may have to pitch it to your boss, or someone else who has the power to approve or reject it. Outside an organisation, you may need to present it to potential partners, investors, clients and customers.

Why a pitch is important

Many people who have ideas undervalue the importance of the pitch. They think, 'Surely a good idea should stand on its own merits'. Well, yes and no. Of course the quality of an idea is important, but so is how you pitch it.

When you are asking someone to embrace an innovative idea, you are asking them to make a decision to change, and change makes people nervous. If you can explain clearly, succinctly and confidently how your idea is going to make things better, it helps a great deal. If, on the other hand, you are nervous and unsure and your pitch is unclear and long-winded, it will be a lot harder for the person listening to feel safe about supporting your idea.

You aren't just selling your *idea*. You are selling *yourself*, because those listening to your pitch will be thinking that if they get involved, they are going to have to work with *you*. So they will be assessing both you and your idea.

A strong pitch can hook someone; a weak one can lose them. Managers need to be convinced and made to feel safe; so do potential customers, investors and partners.

Who should pitch?

If you are the only one involved in creating the idea, then you have to pitch it. But what if several people are involved? How do you decide who should pitch the idea? The question to ask is, 'Who will do the best job?' That won't necessarily be the person who has done the most work to develop the idea. Try to take ego out of it and work out who is able to pitch most clearly and convincingly.

Also, think about any baggage anyone may be carrying. For example, if someone has a history of negative experiences with management in general, or with the person you are pitching to in particular, it's probably best they don't do it. You don't want a good idea to die just because Bob might not get a fair hearing.

What are you trying to achieve?

The first step, before you even start to write your pitch, is to work out exactly what you are trying to do. Think about your audience. Who are they? Someone higher up in your organisation? Or potential investors, customers, or partners?

Think about what they want. Put yourself in their shoes and try to imagine what is going to make them receptive to your idea, and what will scare them off.

When pitching an idea, people often focus too much on how clever it is, and not enough on how it can make the other person's life better. Focus on what your idea can do for the person you are pitching to. If you are pitching to your boss, focus on how your idea can improve the way the organisation does things. If you are pitching to an investor, focus on why it is a good investment. If you are pitching your innovation to a potential customer or client, explain how it can make their life better.

Next, think about what you are trying to get the person to whom you are pitching to *think*, *feel* and *do*.

□ *What do you want your audience to **think**?* If you are pitching to management, you want them to think your idea could help the company and is worth developing. If pitching to an investor, you want them to think the innovation will be successful, and that you are a good businessperson. If pitching to a customer or client, you want to convince them that buying your product or service makes good business sense.

□ *What do you want them to **feel**?* Interested, intrigued, excited, FOMO (fear of missing out). And that you are credible and trustworthy.

□ *What do you want them to **do**?* You want them to take the next step. If you are pitching to your boss, that is probably to commit to taking the next step forward with your idea. If you are pitching to an investor or a customer, you want them to be interested enough to seriously consider getting involved.

Once you have answered these questions, you are ready to start writing your pitch. As you do, keep checking back to make sure that what you plan to say will help you to achieve your aim of getting your audience to think, feel and act in the way you want them to.

How long should your pitch be? If in doubt, make it shorter rather than longer.

You should be able to pitch an idea in thirty seconds if you need to, by explaining clearly how it can make your listener's life better. A fridge, for example, could be pitched in this way:

> It's like a kitchen cupboard that you put food in but it keeps the food cold so that it doesn't go off.

Note there is nothing in the pitch about how the refrigerator actually manages to keep the food cold. Rather, the focus is on how having a fridge will make someone's life better.

There are basically just two things you need to think about when preparing a pitch: *what you say* and *how you say it*. Each aspect is important. A great story, badly told, is not very convincing. A passable story, brilliantly told, can be inspiring. For a good pitch, you need to have good content (what you say) and to deliver it in a way that is engaging (how you say it).

What you say

Think of your pitch as a story. The story begins when you describe a problem or an opportunity. Next, you explain how your idea solves the problem or takes advantage of the opportunity. Finally, you offer your audience a chance to become involved.

First, clearly set out the problem or opportunity. Explain how big it is, what the benefits of tackling it are, and what the costs of ignoring it are.

Second, explain your idea. Use clear, simple language. Think about your audience's level of technical knowledge. Don't use technical or industry-specific jargon, unless you are absolutely sure that everyone you are speaking to will be able to follow it.

It's important to ensure that *everyone* you are pitching to can understand *every word* you say. If you lose someone, you can't expect them to stop you and ask for an explanation. People are often reluctant to admit they don't understand something because they don't want to look stupid. Instead they will sit there in silence, and you will have lost them. So make sure your explanations are clear. Before you do your pitch, test it on someone who has limited technical expertise and make sure they understand every word. If they don't, then make your explanation simpler and clearer.

During your pitch, each time you touch on something technical or complex, check in with your audience to make sure they are still with you. 'Did I explain that clearly?'

That way, if there is any confusion, you can clear it up.

Emphasise *what your idea does* rather than *how it does it*, especially if the 'how' part involves something that is complex and technical. People will be much more excited by: 'These changes in the supply chain will save $50 000 a year' than by a detailed description of how you are going to revamp stock deliveries. Of course you need to explain how your innovation works, but don't get bogged down in detail.

Keep focusing on what it is that your audience wants. Remember, it's not about showing them how clever you are. It's about exciting them with an opportunity that can benefit them. A couple of key statistics about the benefits your innovation may bring would be helpful, but don't drown your audience in figures.

Explain the clever bit. A lot of new ideas have something about them that makes you go 'Wow!' For example, I got a new laptop recently and the bit that makes me go 'wow' is that it has a touchscreen like a tablet. (Of course, by the time you read this, that will probably be old hat.) Work out what the 'wow' bit of your innovative idea is, and allow the audience to experience the excitement of it (without drowning them in jargon).

Explain why it makes sense for your audience to embrace your pitch. Often that will involve explaining to them how implementing your idea is going to save or make them money.

Finally, focus on the opportunity your audience have. Make it really clear to them exactly what it is you want them to *do*, and why it makes sense for them to do it.

Remember, a good pitch has three parts:

1 Explain the problem or opportunity.

2 Explain how your innovative idea solves the problem or takes advantage of the opportunity.

3 Explain why it makes sense for the audience to take the next step.

A word on the language you use: Use spoken English, not written English. The way we write is different from the way we speak. The words, sentence structures and rhythms are all different. A beautifully written sentence can sound stilted and unnatural when spoken aloud. So make sure you practise delivering your pitch aloud, and use words and sentences that sound natural coming out of your mouth. Where necessary, rewrite your pitch.

It is important to sound natural and conversational, not formal and stiff. The more conversational your pitch, the better. All you are doing is telling someone about your idea and why it makes sense for them to give it a go. Speak as you speak every day, not as you think a formal presenter should speak. Don't hide behind overformal language. Be yourself.

How you say it

Once you have worked out what you want to say in your pitch that's it, right? You just go in and say it. Wrong! How you deliver you pitch is just as important as what you say. If you speak confidently, engage your audience and make your points clearly and concisely, then you will have a much greater chance of success than if you are unsure, nervous and waffly.

Good public speakers are not born; they are made. If you work at it, you can become a much better public speaker than you are now. It's not a natural talent; it's a learned skill. It's a cop-out to say, 'I'm just no good at public speaking'. It's like learning the violin. Everyone sounds awful when they start. Then they practise and they get better. Here are some tips.

Respect the fact that a good pitch is hard

If you have finished writing your pitch that doesn't mean it's ready! A good ten-minute pitch should take hours of preparation. When you have it all written out, what you have is a first draft. The way to make it better is to go over it again and again. Not reading it, but *saying* it aloud. From this you:

- learn it, and get comfortable with it
- find ways to improve it.

Each time you go over your pitch, and say it aloud, you should be able to find a way of making it clearer, sharper and more focused. Keep improving it right up to your presentation. Don't just practise the words and emphasis. Practise your commitment to the words, your belief.

Before the real thing, be sure to test your pitch on others and ask them for feedback:

◻ Was there anything they found unclear?

◻ Did they find their attention wandering at any point?

◻ Were they convinced that the idea will work? Would they take the next step?

◻ If not, why not?

Your pitch starts as you walk in the door. As soon as your audience see you, they start to form an impression. So enter the room with confidence and enthusiasm.

Two things can build confidence:

◻ *Preparation*. Make sure you know your pitch (and your innovation) back to front, inside and out.

◻ *Belief*. If you don't believe in your innovation, you probably shouldn't be pitching it.

Nervousness

What if you get nervous? That's okay. You don't need to feel totally confident to give a great pitch. You just need to *act* confident.

It's normal to feel nervous about public speaking. Harnessing the energy those nerves generate can help you to create a vigorous pitch. If you can't control your nerves, though, they can end up controlling you and cause you to sweat, stumble and lose your way, which will make your pitch a lot less effective and distract your audience.

The important thing to remember is that we're not trying to completely eliminate nervousness. Feeling nervous is unpleasant, but normal. What we are just trying to do is to stop those nervous feelings from sabotaging your ability to do an effective pitch.

This is what to do about nerves.

Nervousness before the day

If you feel anxious in the days leading up to the event, either do something productive to improve your pitch, or distract yourself by doing something else. Don't sit and ruminate unproductively. It doesn't help!

The nerves may be a sign that you are underprepared. If so, do more preparation. The better prepared you are, the more confident you will feel, and the less nervous you are likely to get.

If you are feeling nervous but you don't want to or don't have time to work on your pitch, then do something that distracts you. Exercise usually works. Or do some other work, or watch TV or something else. The worst thing you can do is to just sit there and worry. It just increases your stress, drains your energy and makes you feel bad.

Nervousness on the day

This is how to control your nerves before your pitch:

1 *Notice the symptoms.* How do you respond physically when you are nervous? Do you fidget or pace, speak faster, get a dry mouth, drink lots of water, speak with a quiver in your voice? Become aware of your nervous mannerisms.

2 *Control the symptoms.* It's very hard to tell yourself not to feel nervous, but it is possible to control some of your physical responses. When you notice you are

exhibiting a nervous symptom, just make yourself stop doing it. For example, if you pace about when you are nervous, then make yourself sit quietly somewhere. That's not so hard. Slow down and take deep breaths. If you tend to stammer or speak with a quiver in your voice, find someone to talk to. If there's no one around, talk to yourself. Warm your voice up. Speak clearly and calmly. One by one, identify and control your nervous symptoms.

Controlling the symptoms of nervousness often makes us feel calmer. But even if it doesn't, it makes us *look* calmer, and that's vital. The goal isn't to completely eliminate all feelings of nervousness. The goal is to avoid looking and acting nervous.

3 *Bring yourself into the moment.* A lot of nervousness is caused by worrying about the outcome. Will it go well, or will it be a disaster? To distract yourself from such unhelpful thoughts, look and listen. Forget about going over and over your pitch in your head. Focus on the here and now. Look around you and notice what is going on.

4 *Redirect your fear into excitement.* Just before you start your pitch, focus on the opportunity that you have. Think about it. You had an idea, and now you have the chance to convince someone else to help you turn it into reality. Get excited!

Verbal ticks

Many of us are prone to verbal ticks, especially when we're tense. Too often we fall back on 'umm' or 'you know' or some other filler while we work out what to say next. Using verbal ticks too much can distract the audience. They stop thinking about what we are saying and instead start noticing how often we say 'you know'.

Identify any verbal ticks you overuse and make a conscious effort to stop relying on them. For example, if you find that you say 'you know' too much, practise talking without saying it. Slowing down your speech a bit can help. That will help your mind stay ahead of your brain, rather than vice versa (but don't slow down too much).

If it's important, say it like it's important

If you think your innovation is a pretty darn good idea, then don't talk about it in a monotone. I have heard people pitch amazing innovations as if they were reading names out of a phone book. How can you expect your audience to get excited by your innovation if *you* don't sound excited by it?

Communication isn't just about the words you use. The audience takes cues from the *way* we speak. If you say 'This is really important' in a monotone, it's hard to believe. If you think it's important, then say it like it's important!

What you say and *how you say it* have to be compatible. In normal conversation, we match our tone to our content. If you say, 'I nearly got hit bit by a car while crossing the street this morning,' you wouldn't say it calmly. You would say it with energy, like it was a big deal.

If you think your innovation is important, give your words weight and gravitas. Make it *sound* important. Part of preparing a pitch is to go through it and work out when to speak in a conversational style, and when to slow down, speak with intensity and really emphasise something that you want the audience to take in and focus on. Rehearse both what you say *and* the way you will say it.

PowerPoint

'My pitch is ten slides long.'

No, it's not! Your pitch is ten *minutes* long, and in it you are using ten slides to help you to make some of your points. PowerPoint is a tool to illustrate your message. It is not the message.

People try to hide behind PowerPoint, but it doesn't work. There's nowhere to hide. If you are pitching an idea, then you will be judged. Get used to it.

Use PowerPoint where it can help you to illustrate a point better than by talking—for example, using diagrams, pictures, graphs and key bullet points.

Don't fill your slides with too many words. You'll just distract your audience. They will half read the words on the screen while they half-listen to you, and probably won't fully digest either.

This is how to test if you are over-dependent on PowerPoint. Imagine you are just about to start your pitch and the projector blows up. Is that a disaster or just a slight inconvenience? You should be able to continue with your presentation without PowerPoint, and still do a great pitch. If you feel that without PowerPoint you couldn't do your pitch, then you are probably over-dependent upon it.

Fill the room

Begin your pitch with confidence, real or faked. Gather yourself and focus. Speak up and out. Try to fill the room with your voice. Project. Give weight to your words. It's better to be too loud than too soft. Imagine you are speaking to someone who is partially deaf and is right at the back of the room.

Don't rush, but keep the pace up. There's nothing worse than the audience knowing how your sentence is going to finish before you get there.

Use silence. If you have made an important point that you want the audience to remember, pause for a couple seconds to allow your words to sink in. Silence is a great tool for emphasis.

Don't *read* your pitch. *Speak* it. Make eye contact with your audience. Talk *to* them. Remember it's an opportunity. Gather yourself, fill the room, be clear, tell them what's in it for them, and make them want to join you.

After it's done, think about what went well and what didn't. Which bits felt like they really connected with the audience? When did you feel you might have been losing them a bit? Were you asked any questions that suggested that some things you said weren't clear or that you should add something further next time? Treat each pitch as a learning experience and use it to make your next pitch better.

CHECKLIST 10: PITCHING YOUR IDEA

- ▫ Pitching your idea is an important part of the process, so prepare thoroughly.

- ▫ Use clear, simple language that everyone can understand.

- ▫ Don't get over-technical. Focus on what your idea does, not how it does it.

- ▫ Tell a story:

    - – Explain the problem or opportunity.

    - – Explain how your idea solves the problem or takes advantage of the opportunity.

    - – Explain why it makes sense for the audience to take the next step.

- Once you have written a pitch, you have a first draft. To improve it, practise, practise, practise.

- It's okay to be nervous. Recognise your symptoms, and, one by one, control them.

- If you think it's important, speak like it's important.

- Use normal conversational language. Don't be over-formal.

- Fill the room with your voice.

- PowerPoint is not your pitch; it is merely an aid. Don't use text-heavy slides.

Chapter 5

INNOVATION IN YOUR OWN LIFE

Innovation isn't just about thinking up ways to improve your business. You can apply the principles of innovative thinking to any aspect of your life. It's about questioning everything you do, asking yourself if there might be a better way, taking some time to think of ways to improve things, and then implementing your best ideas.

Some people are very innovative in how they do their job or run their business, but much less so in how they lead their life.

How can you be innovative in your life? Once again, by *thinking* of ideas, *valuing* those ideas and then *using* them. Let me give you an example.

I went to a private school in Canberra, and then studied economics and law at Sydney University, mainly because I wasn't sure what else to do. In my final year at university everyone seemed to be aiming for a job at a big corporate law firm, so I tried too and managed to land one. But even before I started I kind of knew that being a corporate lawyer wasn't for me. I realised that although I had had many educational and other opportunities, because I had just gone with the flow and never questioned anything I was going to end up in the wrong place. I had let myself drift into a career that looked good from the outside, but that I was ill suited to.

So for the first time in my life (without even realising I was doing it) I went through the think, value, use process.

Think

I tried to imagine what I would do if I could do anything I wanted to, and I kept coming back to the idea of stand-up comedy. Initially I tried to resist the idea. Stand-up comedy was scary. What if I failed? What if I got heckled? What if people laughed at me? Wait, they were supposed to laugh at me, but what if they laughed at me in a cruel rather than an amused way? Or what if they *didn't* laugh at all?

But as I kept coming back to the idea, I knew it was important. That meant I had to give it some value.

Value

Although the idea of trying to become a comedian terrified me, and I had no confidence that I would be able to do it, I had to give the idea some value and see how big it could get. I didn't want to wake up in fifty years' time and wonder what would have happened if I had only had the guts to give it a crack. I didn't know if the idea of doing stand-up comedy was a good idea or a bad idea, but I knew I wanted to find out how far I could take it. And that meant using the idea.

Use

I tried not to get ahead of myself. The idea of comedy becoming my job didn't even enter my mind. I just concentrated on working out what the next thing to do was, and then doing it. It was pretty obvious that the next thing to do was to write a short comedy routine. After about a week I had something, so the next thing to do was to ring up the Harold Park Hotel in Glebe in Sydney and put my name down for the open mike night.

Making that phone call was actually the hardest bit—even harder than getting up on stage. I think it was hard because, for the first time, I was actually taking responsibility for steering my own life, and that can be scary. Finally I made the call.

And everything good that has happened to me in my career flowed from that. My first routine went okay and I kept at it, trying to write jokes on the weekend and doing gigs for free one or two times a week, until eventually I started getting paid. Then, after a few years, I started to get opportunities to do television and radio work.

It all came from thinking about how I could make my life better, valuing the ideas I had and then using them.

What about you?

Are there areas in your life that could do with some innovation? In your career, your personal life, your work–life balance, your health, or any other area?

Think it all through

Maybe there are areas of your life that could do with a bit less doing and a bit more thinking. What are they? What areas don't feel quite right? Take some time to think about them. Question everything you do and ask yourself if there might be a better way of doing it.

You might want to take a few moments to think about, or write down the answers to, the following questions:

- Are you happy in your job? If not, why not?

- How is your work–life balance? If it's not perfect, how could it be improved?

- What are the things you most enjoy? How much time do you spend doing them? Is there a way to spend more time doing them?

- What are the things you least enjoy? How much time do you spend doing them? Is there a way you could reduce that time?

- What's your definition of success? People talk all the time about 'being successful', but what does 'success' actually mean to you? How do you measure it? By status? By salary? By how high you climb in your career? By how happy you are? By how nice a person you are?

- Once you have defined what success means to you, what could you do to become more successful?

- Think of some things you really want to do that you haven't yet done. Could you do some of them?

- If you could change some things in your life, what would they be?

- Is there some way you could move the life *you are* leading a bit closer to the life you ideally *would like* to be leading?

- Are you as healthy as you would like to be? If not, do you want to do more exercise? What would you do? When would you do it?

- Do you want to change what you eat and drink? How?

Maybe you are making some assumptions about how you should lead your life. For example, some people assume they have no option but to stay in a job they don't like. If that sounds like you, are you *sure* you don't have any other options? Maybe you do. Pursuing them might be *difficult*, but saying that your options are difficult is very different from saying that you have *no* options.

If you have identified some areas in your life that you would like to change, then stop dreaming and start strategising. Take off the soft head, put on the hard head and work out how to get from where you are now to where you want to be.

Thinking about how to be innovative in your own life can be even harder than thinking about how to be innovative in your business. It's something we all too frequently put off, but if we keep doing that, eventually it will be too late.

Take some time to think it all through. It's a worthwhile investment of time. Yes, making changes will probably be difficult, but most things that are worthwhile are.

Give your ideas value

Once you have decided what changes you want to make in your life, actually making them can take a great deal of time and commitment. It's almost inevitable that at some point you will feel that implementing the changes you have thought of is just too hard. If that happens, remember *why* you want to make them. Give your ideas some value!

You might want to:

- grow your ideas. Brainstorm and see what you come up with. Follow the steps outlined in 'Thinking is hard' at the end of chapter 1.

- share them with someone you trust, and see if they can help you to expand them.

- outline the practical steps you would need to take to implement the changes you want to make.

Use your ideas

Make sure you use your ideas. Again, don't freak yourself out by thinking about how many steps there are. Just work out what the next thing to do is, then do it. If your goal is to become a pianist, then the first step is probably to buy or hire a piano, and then to get some lessons.

People often set goals that are so ambitious and far away that they seem unrealistic, and they end up losing motivation. For example, setting a goal of becoming a professional concert pianist is daunting. Even if that is your ultimate aim, first set a closer, more modest goal, like being able to play 'Twinkle, twinkle, little star' by the end of the week. That goal is much more achievable, immediate and within your control.

I never had a goal of being a professional stand-up comedian. My goal was always simply to become a *better* stand-up comedian. That was something I could control, and I figured that if I did that, I would maximise the chances of it becoming a career option.

Just keep working out what the next thing to do is, and then do it. Don't worry about how many steps there are. Just take the *next* step. And then take another one.

CHECKLIST 11: INNOVATING IN YOUR OWN LIFE

- ☐ Are there areas of your own life that could benefit from some innovation?

- ☐ **THINK** about ways in which you would like to change your life.

- ☐ Give your ideas **VALUE**. Treat them like they are important.

- ☐ **USE** your ideas. Work out the next thing to do to grow each idea, then do it. Then repeat the process.

PART II
CREATING AN INNOVATIVE ORGANISATION

In Part I we looked at what individuals can do to be more innovative. Now let's focus on organisations.

- How can an organisation create an innovative workplace culture, in which everyone knows that it is part of their job to think up better ways of doing things?

- How can management ensure that they get access to all the ideas that their staff have?

- How can they set up and run an efficient and effective system to assess those ideas, find the most promising ones, trial them and then implement the best ones?

Chapter 6

HOW SUCCESS AND GROWTH CAN DISCOURAGE INNOVATION

Earlier I suggested that innovation isn't something that only the elite are capable of. It's not just for the super-smart or the super-creative. It's something that we can all learn to do. If you accept that, then it follows that if everyone in an organisation *isn't* trying to come up with better ways of doing things, a resource is being wasted. It's like a factory operating at half capacity.

Organisations should always be trying to improve what they do. If they don't, they run the risk of becoming irrelevant. Often people at the coalface, whether working in a factory or meeting face-to-face with customers and clients, have really good ideas about how to do things better. Some organisations are great at harvesting innovative ideas from *all* of their people and then implementing the best ones.

Most organisations, however, aren't.

When most organisations start they are, almost by definition, innovative. They are doing something new, or at least the people in the organisation are learning and doing new things. When an organisation is new and small, there are new challenges, new opportunities and new problems all the time. To meet those challenges, take advantage of the opportunities and solve the problems, innovative thinking is required.

Then, if those in the organisation do what they do well and/or they are lucky, the organisation grows. As the organisation becomes more established, more systems and processes are put in place. Now when a problem arises it is often the same as, or similar to, a problem that was solved last month or last year. So, rather than someone having to think in an innovative way about how to solve that problem, they instead follow precedent and procedure.

There's nothing wrong with that. In fact, it's smart and efficient, but it means that innovative thinking becomes less of a necessity. As businesses get systematised, the need for everyone to be continually solving problems diminishes. People get out of the habit of being innovative.

As organisations become successful and grow they have to manage more people, more money, and more clients and customers, and far more effort is needed to simply *keep things going*. Best practice is implemented, which helps those in charge control the decision making of those to whom they delegate. Those at lower levels don't always have to work out for themselves what they have to do. Instead, they just refer to, and follow, established practices. While there is still an emphasis on growing the business, it can become scarier to experiment and perhaps fail, because there is so much more to lose now than there was when the business was starting out. If the business is tracking reasonably well, then the status quo can become a comfortable place. Over time, the entrepreneurial spirit with which the business was started is slowly but steadily stifled by systems, processes and bureaucracy.

While there is still room for the exercise of some individual discretion, creativity and expertise, an inevitable part of the growth of an organisation is the increased use of systems and processes, and a decreased reliance on individual innovative thought.

Of course, many companies *talk* about innovation; they include the word in their values statements, they theme conferences around innovation, and management constantly talks about the importance of being innovative. And yet, in large or even medium-sized organisations, it is common to hear complaints from people down the chain that the prevalence of systems and processes has left very little room for them to actually *be* innovative. If they have an idea about a way to improve things, they often feel daunted by the steps they would have to go through to get their idea heard and acted upon. Often they have very little confidence that their ideas would get a fair hearing or have any chance of being implemented.

So there is often a disconnect between the *intentions* of management ('Everyone needs to be innovative!') and what actually happens.

Wouldn't it be better if everyone in an organisation knew that thinking up new and better ways of doing things was part of their job? Wouldn't it be better if, when people had an idea, they knew that there was a clear, credible and transparent process for assessing it — a process that ensured that every idea got a fair hearing, and that the best ones would be trialled and implemented into the business? Wouldn't it be better if everyone in an organisation had faith that if they shared an idea with management, it would be assessed fairly and they would receive feedback about what was going to happen to it? Wouldn't it be better if an organisation's management regularly received innovative and useful ideas from the people who know the organisation best: those who work in it?

The role of management

Whose job is it to generate ideas to improve the business? A lot of people, especially managers, seem to think it is management's job. The more ideas you get, the better your chances are of uncovering some good and useful ideas. The more people whose job it is to have ideas, the more ideas you will get.

To maximise your chances of finding good ideas to improve your business, you should maximise the number of people whose job it is to come up with them. It should be *everyone's* job to be innovative, from the CEO to the receptionist. That, of course, *includes* management, but it is not *limited to* management.

If you want to create a culture that values and encourages innovation, then first there needs to be a recognition that ideas to improve the business can come from *anyone* in that business, from the top to the bottom. If your business makes and sells buttons, then of course some ideas for doing things better are going to come from those who actually do the making and the selling. If you run a mine, then of course ideas are going to come from the miners themselves. Part of every manager's role should be to allow, encourage and empower others to come up with ideas, and to be open to hearing those ideas and objective in assessing them.

That can involve a bit of a mindset change and often requires a manager to try to take their ego out of it. If a manager finds that one of their team has come up with a brilliant idea, they might feel threatened or insecure. 'I'm the boss,' they might think. 'I'm supposed to be the one doing the thinking.'

They should remind themselves that it's all about getting the best ideas and implementing them. It doesn't matter who has them. This is a message that should be repeated and reinforced from the top down.

Management should ensure that everyone is accountable, not only for doing what needs to be done to keep the organisation going today, but also for their contributions to the continual process of change and improvement that is needed to ensure that the organisation will prosper in the future.

Management should ensure that everyone in the organisation knows that they have a responsibility to have, share and grow innovative ideas. That is, they should *motivate* people to be innovative. But motivation in itself is not enough. There also needs to be a *method*—that is, a system that allows and encourages innovation to happen.

Outsourcing creativity

It constantly surprises me how frequently organisations that are full of intelligent people outsource so much of their interesting and creative work.

When organisations are looking to implement a new marketing or advertising campaign, or to identify ways to become more efficient and cut costs, they often go out, rather than down. That is, they engage external advertising companies, management consultants or HR experts to tell them what they should do, but they don't ask the people who actually work in the organisation.

Of course, management consultants, advertising and marketing firms, and HR experts often have good ideas, but why not also harvest ideas internally, from the people who work in the organisation and know it better than anyone else?

For example, before beginning an advertising campaign, management could send an email to everyone in the organisation that says:

> *We are about to embark on a new advertising campaign for product x, and we have a budget of $y. How can we persuade people who don't currently buy x that they should? You guys know our business better than anyone, so please let me know your ideas.*
>
> *You also know our products better than anyone, so what do you think are the features of product x that will most appeal to people? What is the best way to tell people how great x is and boost our sales? We are trying to collect as many ideas as we can, so please send yours in by return email by Friday. Thanks!*

If you do that, the *worst* outcome is that you won't get any ideas that are worth pursuing, but even if that happens, the only cost has been the time it took to write the email and then read through all the replies. And maybe you *will* get some great ideas that you can either develop yourself or pass on to the advertising agency.

In addition, management has sent all staff the powerful and empowering message that they are open to hearing good ideas from anyone.

Why doesn't this sort of thing happen more?

One reason is that once organisations reach a certain size, they usually have systems and practices that are entrenched and rigorously followed. So the procedure for launching a new advertising campaign might be to give the advertising agency a brief, and then two days or two weeks or two months later the advertising agency reports back and the organisation assesses their ideas. If the organisation likes one, they go with it. If they don't, then the agency goes back to the drawing board.

That's not a bad system but there's an unfortunate assumption in it. That is, that the organisation has to outsource the work because they cannot do it themselves.

Of course, advertising agencies have great expertise and experience in their field, but there isn't any reason why someone from *within* the organisation who has been, for example, working on developing a new type of ice cream, can't come up with a brilliant idea or concept to advertise that ice cream. They might not know everything about how to turn that idea into an advertising campaign, but that's fine. The advertising company can do that.

A lot of organisations seem to suffer from a deep lack of confidence in their own ability to think creatively, and so outsource any task that requires creative thinking. Someone in the advertising industry once said to me, 'I love my job. Companies outsource all the interesting things they do to us. Thank goodness they don't keep them and only outsource the boring bits!'

Imagine that a company was trying to work out how to make the role of their receptionist more efficient. What would they do? They might bring in a management consultant to have a look at the receptionist's duties, they might set up a committee, or they might create a flow chart that showed how and when the receptionist's work was done. There is, however, someone who knows more about the receptionist position than anyone, and who might already have some great ideas about how to improve its efficiency. Yet many managers wouldn't think to ask the receptionist.

When discussing ways to break out of habitual thinking, I noted that sometimes the answers are right in front of us, but because we are thinking in a rigid way we don't see them.

Often management underuse their greatest asset, the brains of those who work in their organisation. No one knows more about your organisation, or its clients and customers, than the people who work within it.

So how do you create an organisational culture in which:

□ everyone is encouraged to be innovative

□ management is able to harvest all the ideas that their staff have, and

□ there is an efficient system for assessing, testing, trialling and implementing new ideas?

To be innovative as an individual, I suggested the following process: (1) *think*, (2) *value* and (3) *use*.

To create an innovative culture, an organisation should apply the same three principles:

1 *Think*. Make it clear that thinking of ways to do things better is part of everyone's job.

2 *Value*. Treat everyone's ideas as an important resource.

3 *Use*. Develop ideas with potential, and establish an efficient and inexpensive process to find the ideas that are going to improve your business.

The aim is to get everyone engaged in innovation, and to have an effective and efficient system for harvesting, assessing and using their ideas.

Some years ago I hosted an awards ceremony for the mining industry. The awards were for innovations that improved safety in mines, and a representative for each nominated innovation had to come onstage and explain how their idea worked. Many of those presenting were actual miners, not people from head office or from the safety committee. Many of the innovations had been thought of by those who actually worked in the mines, and their companies had been smart enough to get access to their ideas, and then to develop, test and implement the good ones.

It seems obvious that many of the ideas for ways to make mines safer are going to come from those who actually work in them, just as many ideas to improve the way that hospitals, schools and businesses run will come from those who work in them. Yet it's amazing how often management forgets this and looks elsewhere.

Here are some ways to create a workplace culture that encourages and values innovation.

Chapter 7

HOW DO YOU GET PEOPLE TO THINK?

While the *development* of innovative ideas can take time and money, *having* an idea doesn't cost anything. Sitting down and thinking is free. And that is how innovation always begins—with someone having an idea. So if an organisation has a hundred people, doesn't it make sense to encourage them all to think?

Think back to all of the jobs you have had in your life. How often has a manager said either of these things to you?

Thinking of new ideas to improve the way we do things is a part of your job.

or

You're new. There's lots to learn, but one of the advantages of being new is that you bring fresh eyes. We probably all take things for granted a bit, so if you see anything you think we could do better, please tell me.

If the answer is never, you're not alone. If you want to create an innovative culture, make it clear that thinking of better ways of doing things is part of *everyone's* job. That is, their job isn't just doing the things that have to be done to keep things ticking over *today*. It also involves thinking up ways to improve the business so it will still be relevant and successful in five years' time.

How do you do that? In some roles, being innovative is a natural part of the job. An intrinsic part of the CEO's job, for example, is working out what to change to ensure the company prospers. But further down the food chain, many employees simply 'do their job', rather than questioning whether it could be done better.

That's not because they are incapable of being innovative. It's often because they have never been *asked* to think about ways of improving things, much less *told* that it is an essential part of their job.

Sometimes the reason people don't think about ways to improve the business is that they don't think it is part of their job. Other times people *do* come up with new ideas but don't share them because they have never been told that their ideas are valued and that management wants to hear them. So instead of sharing their ideas, they just let them float away. Often they are convinced that if they *did* try to develop or share an idea, no one would be interested and nothing would happen.

Everyone in an organisation is capable of thinking of ways of doing things better, but you have to encourage them and give them a structure through which to do it.

Make it clear it's part of the job

How do you make it clear to every member of the organisation that part of their job is to think up ways of improving the business?

Of course most of their day should be spent ensuring that today's business is done as well as it possibly can be, but a part of everyone's day should also be devoted to questioning the way things are done and thinking about how they could be done better.

Ensure that being innovative is one of every employee's key performance indicators. That is, part of their job is to come up with ideas to improve the business, and they are accountable for that in just the same way as they are for all their other KPIs.

Create an innovation KPI for everyone that looks something like this:

> *Each month think of, and share, two ideas to improve the way the organisation does things.*

You can choose the target, but two per month is twenty-four a year, which is a good number.

Okay, that sounds nice, but how do you measure an innovation KPI?

Quantity not quality

Often we stress quality over quantity, but if you are trying to up the innovative output of your people, you need to do the opposite.

Emphasise that the innovation KPI is about having and sharing a specific *number* of ideas. It's not about only sharing ideas they think are great. You are asking them to come up with two ideas per month, not two *brilliant* ideas per month. The goal is to get access to as many ideas as possible. If you emphasise to your team that you only want *good* ideas, then you will inhibit them, and many of the ideas they have will never get to you. Employees will come up with an idea but then think, 'No, I can't share that one. It's not good enough'.

Remember, it's difficult to know at first whether an idea is good, great or terrible. Some ideas that start out sounding terrible end up turning into something worthwhile.

If you say, 'I only want you to pitch ideas that are fully formed and ready to be immediately implemented in the business,' then you may miss out on some good ones. People often have an idea and then strike a problem they can't resolve. Make it clear that you want to hear about those ideas too, because someone else might be able to supply the missing piece of the jigsaw that makes the idea workable.

Suggest people develop their ideas as far as they can, but if they get stuck before all the kinks are ironed out, that's okay. You still want to hear about them, because they may contain something valuable. So encourage staff not to be harsh in judging their ideas.

Emphasise that they don't have to come up with an idea that radically transforms the business. Any small incremental improvement is good, because over time those tiny improvements add up and can make a big difference.

Get access to as many ideas as possible. You don't want to miss out on one just because the person who thought of it lacks self-confidence and isn't sure if it's good enough. If you make sure that you get as many ideas as you can, then you will maximise your chances of finding some great ideas.

Keep it simple for staff. Emphasise that only want them to do two things:

1 Generate new ideas to improve the business.

2 Share them with management.

Don't set the bar too high. Just get people to do as much as they can, and then share their idea.

The hardest part is getting people to *start* thinking that innovation is part of their job, especially if they are not used to doing so. Change is always hard, but as the idea that innovation is everyone's responsibility grows and becomes an accepted part of the culture, it should get easier, and eventually become the new normal.

Once you have made innovation a KPI, follow through. If someone doesn't hit their target for ideas submitted, then call them out on it. Make them accountable. It is perfectly legitimate to say to someone at a performance review, 'You've hit your sales targets, your clients love you, you meet deadlines and are easy to work with, but in the past three months you haven't pitched any ideas to help us do things better. And if everyone did that, in five years we'll be in a lot of trouble'.

But, you might be thinking, you can't dream up ideas to a deadline. Ideas come or they don't. You can't conjure up an idea just because it's the end of the month and you have to hit your target.

Actually, you can.

Deadlines are a wonderful way of motivating creativity. Think of the cleverest, most creative and brilliant television shows or movies you have seen. Much, often most, of the creative work was done to a deadline. There would have been deadlines on writing and rewriting the script, on filming each scene and on editing it into its final form. Charles Dickens serialised many of his novels and had to write each part to a deadline.

We have all faced tasks we have had to finish by a certain time—writing a report, preparing a speech, writing an essay, studying for an exam. Two weeks before the deadline we act as if we have all the time in the world. A few days before the work is due we realise we have actually left it much too late and there is no way we will have enough time to do it properly. We panic, we work really hard … and get it done. And that work often includes lots of creativity. I have already talked about the advertising industry. They have to be creative to deadline. Clients don't say, 'We need a thirty-second ad for our new car. Obviously, we can't put any sort of deadline on you having creative ideas, so just take as long as you need. A week, a month, a year, whatever. I know you can't rush these things'. No. They say, 'We need it in a week'.

I used to do an evening radio show five nights a week from 7 pm to 10 pm. It was almost all talk, and by the time I got to the studio in the afternoon, most of the news of the day had already been covered by earlier programs. My producer and I had to try to think up original stories, or new angles on the stories that had already been covered. Some days it was easy, but sometimes it was really hard. As our deadline loomed we knew we had to come up with something interesting, or we would have a big block of nothing in the middle of the show. And you know what? Day in, day out, for six years, we *always* came up with something. I didn't have all my ideas because I was brilliant. I had them because I had to.

The motivation for staff to generate innovative ideas involves a mixture of stick and carrot. The carrot: by encouraging staff to think up ideas and share them, you set them a task that is challenging, interesting, creative and potentially exciting, and thereby empower them. The stick is that innovation is one of their KPIs, so they know they are accountable for it in the same way as they are for all their other KPI's. This factor, especially, helps with motivation when it gets hard. And thinking of new ideas almost always does get hard, so motivation is important.

Managers need motivation, too, so they can also be set a KPI that makes them accountable for encouraging, harvesting and passing on the ideas of their staff. For example:

You are responsible for encouraging your team to generate and pitch innovative ideas to you, and for conducting an initial assessment of those ideas before passing them on to the innovation committee.

A manager can be accountable not just, for example, for the *sales* output of the team, but also for the *innovative* output of the team. Just as a quarterly target may be set for sales, a target can also be set for how many ideas a manager's team should come up with.

CHECKLIST 12: CREATING AN INNOVATIVE CULTURE

- ☐ Make innovation a KPI for everyone. For example, 'Come up with two new ideas each month to improve the way we do things'.

- ☐ Don't set the bar too high by saying you only want to hear *good* ideas. Get access to as many ideas as possible.

- ☐ Deadlines are a great way to inspire creative thinking.

Chapter 8

IF YOU THINK INNOVATION IS IMPORTANT, ACT LIKE IT'S IMPORTANT

If you believe the claims made in many organisations' mission statements and core values, on their websites and at conferences and meetings, you would assume they value innovation highly. Often, however, when you look deeper, you get a suspicion that while companies work hard to *look like* they are innovative in every way they can, many are ignoring some very simple opportunities to create an innovative workforce.

Innovation campaigns

Even companies that claim they are committed to innovation often treat it as an extra—that is, as icing rather than the cake itself. For example, they might run an innovation campaign for a month in which they invite staff to submit an idea to improve the organisation, and reward those who come up with the best ideas. But then the campaign ends and life goes back to normal. The message sent is that innovation is an add-on—it's not core business.

Innovation should be something we do *all the time*, not just for one month a year. If you think innovation is important, then act like it's important. Don't send the message that it is something the organisation should just focus on *sometimes*. Organisations don't run campaigns where everyone is urged to focus on sales for a month, because everyone knows they are supposed to focus on sales all the time.

Running a campaign to encourage innovation is better than doing nothing, but it's not nearly as good as entrenching innovation as a part of normal, daily business.

Tell people what you want them to do

There is a big difference between motivation and instruction.

Motivation isn't that hard. You just say, 'Innovation is very important. We pride ourselves on being innovative and we embed innovation in everything we do. Everyone in our organisation needs to be constantly on the lookout for ways to be innovative'.

That's a good message, and most people who hear it will think, 'Yeah! Right on!' But it's not telling anyone what to do *to be* innovative. So when staff get back to their desks, or wherever they work, because they haven't been clearly told what to *do*, it's likely that nothing much will change.

Don't just *talk* about innovation being important. Tell people what to do. If you want to create an innovative culture (or any sort of culture), you have to be really clear about exactly what it is you want people to do differently, because instruction is more useful than motivation.

This is true in most areas. You can tell your children *why* cleaning their teeth is important (motivation), but what will really make a difference is giving them a very clear and simple instruction: 'Clean your teeth for one minute every morning after breakfast and every evening before you go to bed.' Or whatever. I'm no dentist.

So if you want to create a more innovative culture, what should you tell people to do?

□ As discussed in chapter 7, ask them to achieve a monthly quota of new ideas to improve the business.

□ Ask them to spend some time each week exploring where there may be opportunities for innovation. Tell them to look out for, and take note of, things they suspect might not be perfect and to think about ways to make them better.

□ Ask them to spend ten minutes each day thinking about how to take advantage of the opportunities they identify.

□ Suggest they question everything they do, and ask, 'Might there be a better way of doing it?'

□ Ask them to identify what assumptions they are making about the business, about their customers, about the market and about their competitors. Urge them to question those assumptions.

□ Encourage them to think like their customers and clients. Ask, 'How can we make life easier and better for our customers and clients?'

□ Have them develop their ideas as far as they can before they pitch them.

- Urge them not to judge their ideas too quickly. Emphasise that you just want them to have ideas. They don't have to be brilliant ideas.

- Ask them to collaborate if they get stuck when developing an idea.

- Keep reminding your team in as many different ways as you can that *innovation is important*. For example:

  - Talk about it in meetings.

  - On random days send around an email that says something like, 'Have you spent ten minutes today thinking about how to make this organisation better? If not, make sure you do!'

  - Put up posters reminding people of what you want them to do.

Consider instituting 'innovation time', a period in the week during which people concentrate on generating and developing new ideas. You have probably heard of companies that permit employees to work on their own projects during work time. Google has allowed employees one day a week to do this, and claims that ideas developed in that time are responsible for the company's 'most significant advances'.

You don't have to go as far as that and allow 20 per cent of an employee's time to be used for innovation, but what about an hour a week, or even half an hour? Here are some of the benefits of doing so:

- Staff might devise, develop and share ideas that will improve your business and make or save the organisation money.

- Management will send a clear message to staff that they are committed to *doing* innovation, not just *talking* about it.

▫ By instituting innovation time, management will get people into the habit of thinking independently, challenging norms, and coming up with and developing their own ideas. There may be spin-off benefits. Once staff are used to thinking in this way, then it might not just be in their weekly half-hour of innovation time that they come up with new ideas. They will be more likely to have their eyes and brain open for ways to take advantage of opportunities for innovation *all* the time.

If you do implement innovation time, how do you make sure that everyone uses it? It's easy to say, 'You should all spend half an hour a week thinking about how to make the business better'. Everyone will loudly agree, set off with the best intentions, and then get swamped with work they think is more urgent.

'It's a fantastic idea,' they will explain. 'It was just that I was really busy and didn't get around to it *this* week.' And they'll mean it. The problem is that *every* week is really busy, and innovation time will usually be the first thing that gets dropped.

If you are determined to embed innovative thinking in your organisation:

1 Make innovation a KPI, as discussed in chapter 7. If people know they are accountable for their innovative output, then they are more likely to make time for it.

2 Institutionalise innovation time. Have everyone nominate their own half-hour or hour block. Make sure that time is in everyone's diary, as immoveable as any other appointment.

How much direction do you give?

When encouraging people to be innovative, you can either direct them to come up with *any* idea to improve the business, or be more specific in your direction. There may be a particular area that you want people to focus on. You may think the sales team is really working well but things are a little stale in marketing. In that case, you might want to urge everyone to think up ideas to improve things in the marketing department. The following month you may want to direct your team to focus on a different area, and the month after that on a different one again.

Alternatively, you might want to get those who work in marketing to focus on coming up with innovative ideas for marketing and those in sales to focus on sales. Or maybe you would get some fresh ideas if you asked the sales people to focus on ways to improve marketing and the marketing people to think of ideas for the sales team. Try it all out, and see what works best.

What if someone says 'I can't'?

Sometimes people will be so fixed in their habits, and so lacking in confidence in their ability to think in a different way, that they will believe they are incapable of coming up with original ideas.

They're not.

Yes, everyone has different abilities, and some people are more adept at solving problems and exploring new possibilities than others, but very few people are incapable of thinking up new ideas.

As with most things, the hardest part is beginning. Usually, the more you do it, the better you get. Once someone comes up with one idea and realises they can do it, then the next idea is often easier to find.

So encourage your team. Take the pressure off by assuring them their idea doesn't have to be great, or even good. It just has to be ... something. Remind them that innovation is part of their job, and when they do come up with something, be encouraging.

CHECKLIST 13: CREATING AN INNOVATIVE WORKFORCE

- Don't treat innovation as an extra. Embed it and treat it as core business.

- Make it really clear what you want your people to *do*. Keep reminding them of practical things they can do that will help them to be innovative.

- Consider introducing 'innovation time'.

- Think about what areas you want your team to focus their innovative effort on.

- Those who think they can't be innovative might just lack confidence, not ability.

Chapter 9

VALUING IDEAS

When someone comes up with an idea, the way in which they are treated by management is very important. If management treats people and their ideas with respect, then those people are much more likely to come back and share more ideas.

Think about the psychology of it. When people are challenged to come up with innovative ideas, they may feel unsure of their ability to do so. When they do come up with an idea, they will probably feel a bit proud, a bit excited, but also still a bit uncertain and nervous. They won't be sure their idea is any good, and they'll wonder how it will be received.

So they will feel vulnerable. Treat them gently. Regardless of the *quality* of their idea, thank them for going to the *effort* of producing it and for having the *courage* to share it.

Make sure they feel their contribution is valued. If they have a good experience with the first idea they share, then it's far more likely they will come back with more. And the next one could be the idea that is really valuable. If they have a bad experience, then they won't want to go through the process again.

Pitch ideas to a person, not an email address

Earlier I suggested that organisations about to embark on, for example, a new advertising campaign, should request staff to submit ideas via email. That's a great way to harvest ideas for specific campaigns when timeframes are tight, but if you want to set up a pipeline to access innovative ideas from staff on a regular basis, then the best way to do it is to allow them to pitch their ideas in person.

A lot of organisations direct their employees to submit their ideas to a specific email address they have set up, often called something like ideas@ourorganisation.com. It's the electronic equivalent of the suggestion box.

I don't like this practice. It's impersonal. Often people don't even know the name of the person who will be sitting in judgement of their idea. If you think innovation is important, act like it's important and have your people pitch their idea to a person, not an email address.

Managers should pick an hour or a half-hour each week when they can be available and say to their team, 'Every Wednesday between three and four I will be available. I will schedule no appointments. I'll take no phone calls. I'll be at my desk working, but as soon as anyone comes in you will have my full attention. That is the time I want you to come in and pitch me new ideas. And if no one comes, I'll be sad.'

By making that commitment (and, of course, keeping it) the manager sends a strong message that they think innovation is important. It's only half an hour or an hour a week, and if you get one decent idea every couple of months from it, it will probably end up being time very well spent.

There are several advantages to having people pitch their ideas in person. If the pitcher is hesitant and unsure, then the manager can help to tease out their idea. The manager can ask questions about things that weren't covered in the pitch. Importantly, at the end of the pitch the manager can ensure the staff member feels valued and that the experience has been a positive one for them.

If that sounds a bit touchy-feely, remember what your goal is: to get access to as many ideas as possible. The more ideas you access, the more likely you are to discover the one (or two or three) that will significantly improve your business. Employees who find pitching an idea to be a positive experience will be more likely to come back and pitch another one. If, on the other hand, their experience is negative, they will be more reluctant to come back and try again. Not only that, they may tell others about their negative experience and discourage *them* from sharing their ideas.

If you are worried about how much time this might take, consider this: anyone should be able to pitch you an idea in one to two minutes, or in a couple of hundred words. So, if you manage ten people and each one has a KPI of two innovative ideas per month, that means you will need to listen to twenty pitches each month. If you limit the pitches to two minutes each and allow another five minutes for discussion and evaluation, that should only take two hours and twenty minutes a month, or about five to seven minutes a day.

Ask people to address the following questions in their pitches:

◻ What is the problem you are solving or the opportunity you are taking advantage of?

◻ What does your innovation do? How does it solve the problem or take advantage of the opportunity?

◻ How will it make things better? Is it going to save or make more money than it costs?

Thank people for bad ideas

If someone pitches you the worst idea in the world, what should you do? Laugh at them? No!

Whenever someone is pitching an idea to you, be gentle. Don't judge their idea too quickly. People treat their new ideas a bit like they treat babies. They are proud of them, nervous about how they are going to make their way in the world, fiercely protective of them and quick to take offence if someone criticises them.

So tread carefully.

When someone pitches you an idea, ask questions and work out what would need to be done next to move the idea forward. If the idea has flaws, don't leap on them. Raise them gently and ask if the pitcher has thought about the issue and can see a way around it. Maybe they need to go away and think about it. If so, set a time to speak again. Maybe they need to collaborate with someone who has skills they don't. If they do, try to steer them in the right direction.

Don't expect any idea to be perfect when it is first pitched. Look for those with the potential to grow into something.

If someone pitches you a really bad idea, thank them for their effort in thinking of it, and for having the courage to pitch it, and reserve judgement for a day or two. Think it over. Are you *sure* the idea isn't a goer? Could anything be done to overcome its problems? Is there any part of the idea that might be useful if applied elsewhere?

If you come to the conclusion that the idea really isn't useful, then talk to the person who pitched it. Point out the problems, and invite them to think about whether they can solve them, or to think of another idea.

It comes back to how you view success and failure. Sorting through lots of ideas that aren't going anywhere is an unavoidable part of getting to the good ideas, so every time you get a bad idea pitched to you, try to think, 'Good! I'm one idea closer to a good one!'

The greater the number of innovative ideas you have access to, the greater the chances that you will find some you can use to improve the way you do things. If you are getting a lot of ideas pitched, that in itself is success.

Anyone who pitches you a bad idea hasn't failed. They are on the right track. It is the person who hasn't bothered to come up with any ideas who has failed.

Be sure to thank your team for their efforts in generating innovative ideas, even if they are not fruitful. You don't have to be motivated by politeness. It's self-interest. If people are made to feel their contribution is valued, then they are more likely to increase their efforts.

CHECKLIST 14: VALUING OTHER PEOPLE'S IDEAS

- ☐ People feel insecure when they are sharing a new idea, so treat them gently.

- ☐ Get people to pitch ideas to a person, not an email address.

- ☐ Thank people for bad ideas, because then they might come back with a good one.

- ☐ The more ideas you get access to, the greater the chances that you will find some good ones.

Chapter 10

USING IDEAS

Once you have harvested ideas from your staff, what do you do with them? You need a structured process that enables you to find the good ideas that will help your business, and then you need to implement those ideas.

When organisations get excited about innovation and run an innovation campaign encouraging everyone to submit ideas, they often don't pay enough attention to the back end. If 112 ideas to improve the business are submitted, what is going to happen to them? Who has responsibility for assessing those ideas and taking the good ones further? What criteria will they use to determine which ideas should be developed further? How *many* of the 112 ideas will be further developed? How will that further development occur? What will the budget be?

Even big companies with lots of resources struggle with this. They run a campaign, rack up all these ideas, and then give them all to Greg to do whatever comes next. No one has thought about how long it will take Greg to go through all those ideas, and he is already busy, so he doesn't quite get around to it, and then after a couple of months someone asks, 'Hey Greg, what happened to all those ideas from the innovation campaign?' and Greg says, 'Oh yeah, um... yeah, I'm going to get to them soon'.

Meanwhile each of the 112 people who went to the trouble of pitching their ideas is wondering why they never heard anything back, and why none of the ideas submitted seem to have gone anywhere. And they begin to wonder why they spent all that precious time thinking up ideas to improve the organisation if nothing was ever going to be done with them. Eventually they become cynical, and they promise themselves that next time they are asked to submit an idea, they won't waste their time.

People won't become disengaged just because you don't use their ideas. As long as you give them clear feedback about *why* their idea isn't being used, most will understand and try again.

They *will* become disengaged, however, if they feel that the whole thing has been a waste of time, that the organisation was never fully committed to following through, and that their effort wasn't appreciated or respected.

There is no point encouraging your people to be innovative if you are not committed to the back end — that is, to assessing the ideas you get, identifying those most likely to make a difference, trialling them and then, if they work, implementing them.

That takes an investment of time and money, but if you implement even one or two good ideas it could result in considerable payback.

So after you collect ideas from staff, what should you do next?

Set up a process

When you implement a new focus on innovation, don't just focus on the front end, the creation of ideas. Think about how it is going to work right through from the creation of ideas to the implementation of the best ones. It is important to set up a transparent, clear and credible system for assessing new ideas.

The first thing to work out is this: once ideas are pitched, what happens next?

In a small organisation, the idea will probably be pitched to the owner or manager of the business, so it is up to him or her to make an assessment of the merits of the idea, and to decide whether it is worth developing it further.

What about in a bigger organisation? Does the manager to whom the idea is pitched make an initial assessment, then send it on to another individual or to a committee with a recommendation? Or do individual managers have autonomy to make decisions about which ideas they want to develop further?

If all ideas are directed to one person for further assessment, has sufficient time been set aside for them to take on the extra responsibility, or are they expected to do it in addition to their existing duties? If the latter, is there a risk that they end up putting off this task in favour of more urgent ones? Try to design a system that ensures ideas are assessed quickly. Perhaps you should include time limits — for example, requiring that a decision be made within five working days of receipt.

If ideas are directed to a committee for assessment, make sure the committee meets regularly and that it isn't too big.

What is the process when new ideas are received by the individual or committee responsible for assessing them? Is a written proposal assessed, or does the person who produced the idea pitch it in person? The former may be quicker, but it doesn't allow committee members the opportunity to ask questions.

Before you get too far into the assessment process, look through all the ideas. Are there ideas that address the same problem or opportunity? Are there ideas that are similar or that overlap in some way? If so, group them together and make sure they are assessed together. Perhaps you will find that a successful innovation will involve using a combination of idea A, idea B and idea C.

What threshold test must an idea pass before the organisation commits to taking it further? It could be something like this:

The three best ideas submitted each month, as decided by the innovation committee, will be developed further, using time and money up to a value of $500 each. The idea will then be reassessed by the committee, who will determine whether there are sufficient prospects of success to justify further development or a trial.

Or this:

Any idea determined by the innovation committee to have a reasonable prospect of improving an aspect of the organisation's business, and of being used by the organisation in its day-to-day business, will be developed further using resources the committee deems appropriate, bearing in mind the committee's annual budget.

This first test simply requires that an innovative idea be one of the best three received that month. The second test sets two criteria: (1) that the idea has a good chance of improving the business, and (2) that it is likely to be adopted. So an idea that looks like it might improve a part of the business, but could be very expensive to implement and run, might satisfy the first part of the test but not the second.

Make sure you establish a clearly defined test to guarantee consistency and transparency.

Work out what options are available to the decision-maker, and make sure there aren't too many. Keep it simple. Maybe they just need three options. They can:

1   reject the idea

2   recommend developing the idea further

3 send the idea back to the source, advising them of specific work to do. For example, 'We think your idea has potential, but we are unsure how it would be implemented. Are you able to explain this further? It might be useful to collaborate with Chris on this'.

Ideas that are going further

If a decision is made to progress an idea further, what then?

1 Work out what needs to be done next to develop the idea, and then do it. Try to do it on a small scale, and as cheaply as you can. If you have a budget to develop an idea, then think hard about how to use it most effectively. If you have, say, five ideas that you have decided to develop, advance them in small steps. After each step, assess the results and decide whether it's worth investing more time and money. Take small steps and keep reassessing.

2 Look for opportunities to collaborate. Perhaps other people within the organisation can help to develop the idea. Work out what sort of expertise is needed, and who within the organisation might be best able to supply it. Then get that person to look at the idea and contribute what they can.

   If innovation is a KPI for everyone, then make it clear that those who collaborate with others to help them to grow their ideas aren't doing something *extra* on top of their job. They are doing their job. At a performance review, a person who has collaborated with two or three others to help them develop their ideas should get credit, just as someone who exceeds a sales target does.

3 Give each project a sense of urgency. Work out what the next thing that needs to be done to develop this idea is, then put a deadline on doing it.

4 Keep the person who had the idea involved in the development process. Let them know what's going on and what the next stage is. If they are ignored and kept in the dark, they might feel resentful and therefore not want to share their next idea. Besides, they probably know more about their idea than anyone else, so they are likely to be useful when developing it.

5 Enshrine accountability in the process. Don't let time limits drift and outcomes remain merely theoretical. For example: 'This seems to be a good idea and has potential. Some further development is needed.' This sort of assessment doesn't *do* anything. If an idea is assessed as having potential, then make sure the decision-maker indicates *what* has to be done next, *when* it should happen and *who* is responsible for doing it.

With respect to the *who*, does the responsibility for taking the idea further rest with a member of the innovation committee, with the person who originated the idea or with someone else? Or does the originator work *with* a member of the innovation committee? Work it out and make sure it is crystal clear to all.

In bigger organisations, think about how centralised or decentralised you want the decision making to be. Do you want individual managers to have autonomy to develop their own team's ideas, and their own budget for doing so? Or do you want all ideas to go to a central decision-making committee?

Ideas that are not going further

What should you do about the ideas that aren't going to go any further?

They fall into two categories: those the decision-maker thinks are never going to get anywhere, and those that cannot be developed in their current form but may, if some problems can be solved, be developed later.

If someone's idea isn't going to be developed, it's important to let them know as soon as possible. Don't leave them in limbo. It can damage confidence and morale if people feel that their idea has mysteriously disappeared up the chain and they never hear back.

Again, it's better to give feedback in person rather than via email. It need take only a few minutes. Give them honest, but not harsh, feedback. Tell them what you liked about their idea, then point out what you think the problems are. Explain why it isn't going any further and invite them to submit another idea soon. Most importantly, thank them for sharing their idea. It's a simple thing, but it has a big effect.

If you think that the idea has problems but that if they can be solved it may still have potential, share your thoughts and invite the person to have another go. Suggest other people with whom they might be able to usefully collaborate.

It's far better to give feedback in person, but if you have to do it by email, then make it personal and specific. Don't just send a form letter. Clearly set out the reasons why the idea isn't going further. Doing this will probably take as long as talking to the person directly, so why not do it face to face? If you think innovation is important, then act like it is important. Think of the time spent as an investment that will encourage future ideas.

Commit!

If you work in a small business, the whole process will probably be a lot less formal, but don't let the back end slide. Commit some time every fortnight to reviewing new ideas and working out which ones are worthy of further exploration, and what the next step should be. Make sure you give feedback and praise. Without them, ideas might stop coming.

In medium and large organisations, you might consider investing in innovation by making someone in upper management responsible for your innovation systems, and formalising their commitment of time so, for example, 20 per cent of their time is devoted to innovation (or 40 per cent or 60 per cent). This person would be responsible for all the innovation systems that harvest, assess, trial and implement new ideas.

If a business has ten partners or managers, that's a total of fifty management work days per week. How many of those fifty days do you want to commit to innovation? If one person devotes two days a week to innovation, that's two out of fifty days, or just 4 per cent of the total management time. Is that the right amount? Too much? Too little? It's all very well to *talk* about how committed you are to innovation, but the test of commitment is not what you *say*, it's what you *do*.

Find the end point of each idea

The aim of all this is to find the end point of every idea. Those involved in the decision-making process should be able to identify the end point of each idea they have seen or heard. For example: 'Idea A didn't get past the committee stage because we believed it would cost more to implement than it would save us. Idea B was trialled but didn't produce the benefits we were hoping for. Idea C was successfully trialled and is now being rolled out across the organisation.'

CHECKLIST 15: USING IDEAS

- ☐ Have a clear process for assessing ideas. Work out exactly how it will work.

- ☐ Invest sufficient time and money in the idea development process so you can find the end point of each idea.

- ☐ When an idea is developed, don't let it drift. Make someone accountable for doing the next thing within a certain time frame.

- ☐ Keep the person who had the idea in the loop. Let them know what is happening.

- ☐ Consider making someone formally responsible for the organisation's innovation systems.

Chapter 11

REACH RIGHT DOWN

When management is searching for new ideas for a marketing campaign, or for a strategy, or for ideas to increase sales or to cut costs, or for a new slogan, why don't they more often seek the input of the people who know the most about the organisation—the staff?

Most organisations, big or small, could benefit if management reached down for ideas more regularly. If there is a problem to be solved, or a strategy to be created, the first step should be to get a broad range of ideas on the table. Then you can work out what the best ones are. Who better to provide those ideas than those who work within the organisation?

Imagine two businesses, a restaurant and a large electrical goods retailer. Both are experiencing declining sales and need a strategy to revitalise their business. Both could benefit by first asking everyone who works in the business to contribute ideas. Doing so doesn't take a lot of resources. All they need do is send out a general email:

> *We are looking to grow the business and win more customers, and would appreciate it if you took some time to think about ways we might achieve this.*
>
> *Please think about it and pass on your ideas. If you can't think of any solutions, then perhaps you can instead identify any problems you think we have. What isn't working perfectly? In what areas could our processes be improved? Which of our systems are inefficient? What irritates our customers? Please share your ideas or thoughts with your manager, or by emailing me, by the end of the month.*

I mentioned earlier that getting people to pitch ideas in person is generally the best option, but if you want to get a lot of ideas on the table quickly, make it as easy as possible for people to submit them; they can pitch it in person, send an email or write it on the back of a sandwich wrapper. It doesn't matter.

Extra incentives can be created, such as offering prizes for the best ideas, but in a culture where innovation is embedded as core business, and not seen as something extra, that shouldn't be necessary.

The worst outcome would be that the organisation received no usable ideas. But even if that happened, management will have sent a strong, positive message that innovation is everyone's job.

The best outcome would be that the organisation accessed some really good ideas that helped them to turn their fortunes around. The best ideas for innovation don't always come from the top. People at lower levels of an organisation often have really good ideas about what is going wrong. They are the ones who speak to the customers, who hear what is holding them back, and who know what systems are clumsy and inefficient, because they deal with them every day. It's hard for management to maintain a clear view of everything. Staff can operate as their eyes and ears. Management simply needs to give them the opportunity to be heard.

Good leadership is not just about having good ideas and making decisions. It's also about empowering others to do the same, and creating an environment that encourages them to do so. It's silly to think that no one below a certain level is capable of coming up with ideas to improve the business.

If you want to create an innovative culture, be brave enough to ask those below for their input. If they have good ideas, then use them. By collecting as many ideas as you can before making a decision, you will have more options to choose from and should be able to make better decisions. Of course, you don't want the process to become cumbersome, but if you ask staff for ideas about a new business strategy and fifty people reply, reviewing that information is likely to help you make a better decision. Even if you disagree with all their ideas, the process of reviewing them will, in all likelihood, help you to clarify your own thoughts.

When an organisation fails to harvest ideas from its staff, it is the organisation that misses out.

If you're going to do this, make sure you send everyone who submits a suggestion a note of thanks. Let everyone know what your eventual decision is, and the reasons why you made it. Everyone who contributes deserves acknowledgement.

Take advantage of every opportunity to harvest ideas from your staff. For example, performance appraisals involve the organisation giving feedback to the employee. Why not turn it around and make a part of the appraisal about the *employee* giving feedback to the *organisation*. Ask the employee for suggestions on what the organisation could do better. Find out what frustrates them about the organisation, what systems and procedures are clumsy and inefficient and waste their time, what makes their job harder, and what strategies they think are misguided. Harvest as many of their ideas as often as you can.

Look for patterns. If you get feedback from employees and six out of ten people say they think there are too many meetings that don't seem to achieve anything, maybe they have a point. At the very least, it suggests that you should take a closer look at what's going on in those meetings.

Similarly, when someone is leaving the organisation, voluntarily or involuntarily, meet with them and ask them to tell you all the things the organisation is doing wrong. It's a great opportunity to get some open and honest feedback, so don't waste it.

Finally, be aware of the ways in which the flow of ideas can be blocked. Here are the three most common blocks:

- **Block 1.** People don't think it's part of their job to generate innovative ideas.

  Solution: Make it clear to everyone that innovation is an important part of their job. Make it a KPI, so they are accountable.

- **Block 2.** People have ideas but don't feel motivated to share them.

  Solution: Send strong and frequent messages that you want and value their ideas. Give feedback and thanks. Follow through and find the end point of every idea.

- **Block 3.** People share their ideas with management, but then none of the ideas ever get developed.

  Solution: Set up a clear, thorough and workable process for assessing, filtering and trialling ideas, and ensuring that the ones most likely to improve your business are used. Ensure that sufficient resources are devoted to the back end, and enshrine accountability.

CHECKLIST 16: REACHING DOWN

- ☐ When making big decisions about your business, reach right down to harvest ideas from staff.

- ☐ Get feedback from staff about what is working well in the organisation and what isn't.

- ☐ Look out for innovation blockages, and fix them.

CONCLUSION: THE ADVENTURE OF INNOVATION

I once had a boss who gave me a task. I worked really hard and finished most of it, but there was one thing I didn't understand. I went into his office, told him my problem and asked him if he could explain it.

'No,' he replied.

'Oh,' I said, taken aback. 'Umm, why not?'

'Because you haven't thought about it.'

'Yes, I have.'

'Well, think about it some more,' he said.

I retreated to my office and felt sorry for myself. Then I started to think about the thing I didn't understand. I thought and thought and thought, and eventually I figured it out. I realised that I hadn't really tried very hard to work it out for myself before giving up and asking my boss. He had been right when he said I hadn't thought about it, and instead of spoon-feeding me, he had called me out on my intellectual laziness.

I learned two valuable lessons that day. One was that often, when we feel like we are working really hard, we are not actually *thinking* that hard at all.

The second was that when we do take a few moments to step back and *really* start thinking, we can solve many of our problems.

Innovation isn't easy. But it's not something that only geniuses can do, either. When it comes to innovation (and many other things) brilliance is overrated, and determination and hard work are underrated.

For the most part, I have argued that you should try to be innovative because it will be good for your business, but there's another reason that innovation is a good thing to do.

It's an adventure.

As a result of human innovation, the lives of many of us today are safer and more comfortable than human lives have ever been. That's great, but perhaps one result is that it's a bit harder to have adventures than it used to be. Back in the old days, when we humans had to go out and hunt for food, every day was an adventure. Now things are more predictable.

Every innovator is on an adventure. The adventure of ideas. They start with a thought, and then they take that idea out of their head and into the world to see how big they can grow it. It is a challenge and a test. It's not easy, but it is exciting, and rarely dull. It's good for us.

There are many reasons why innovation is good *business*, but it can also be good *life*. I hope you decide to embark on the adventure of innovation.

NOTES

In writing this book, I have drawn on various blog posts and articles I have written over the years, and on keynote presentations I have given on innovation. Other sources include the following.

Preface

Information about the original ABC-TV series *The Inventors* was obtained from the Australian Screen website.

Throughout the book, information about the inventors and inventions that appeared on *The New Inventors* came from three sources: my own memory, my notes and the show's own website, accessed through abc.net.au. The website survives to this day (or at least to the date of publication) and has lots of information about all the featured inventors and their inventions so, if you are curious, browse away. There's some great stuff there.

Introduction

Check online for the many definitions of *innovation*, *invention*, *innovator* and *inventor*.

Chapter 1

I heard Professor Rosabeth Moss Kantor talk about habitual thinking (and many other things) at the Australian Chambers Business Congress in Melbourne on 16 August 2012.

Question everything

The story of Suvir Merchandani and the costs of printer's ink can be found by searching for:

'India teen tells US how to save $400 million by changing font'

Source: *The Hindu*

'Suvir Mirchandani tells US government how to save £240m — just by changing their font'

Source: *The Independent*

What assumptions are you making?

Information on how Air Canada and IBM enabled customers to view the airline's content on their own device can be found by searching for:

'Air Canada rouge soars ahead with wireless in-flight entertainment service'

Source: IBM

Is the answer in your data?

The story of Tacoma Zoo analysing weather and attendance can be found by searching for:

'How a Tacoma Zoo Improved Staffing, Visitor Experience with Big Data'

Source: *Building a Smarter Planet*

Information on Cincinnati Zoo's analysis of how its visitors spent money is collected in:

'Business Intelligence Helps the Cincinnati Zoo Work Smarter',
Source: *Essentials of Management Information Systems 11th edn*, ch. 11, case 4 by Kenneth C. Laudon and Jane P. Laudon (via course materials from Mercer University)

Upworthy's analysis of its readers' habits is discussed in:

'How Upworthy is using data to move beyond clickbait and curation'
Source: *NiemanLab*

I became aware of enLighten through my involvement with the Australian Cleantech Competition (later the Australian Technologies Competition), run by that great champion of Australian innovation John O'Brien. Steve Cahill, the CEO of enLighten Australia, kindly reviewed the section on the company.

Think like a customer or client

I first heard of Meat Pack from technology entrepreneur and speaker Mick Luibinskis. The story of Meat Pack's Hijack campaign is found on the thinkwithgoogle website.

Plan for failure

Information on why there are ashtrays in planes is found in:

'Why Airplanes Still Have Ashtrays in the Bathrooms'
Source: *Gizmodo*

'Why aeroplanes still have ashtrays in the bathroom'
Source: *Business Insider Australia*

'If You Can't Smoke on Planes, Why Are There Still Ashtrays?'
Source: *Mental Floss*

Get bored

Dr Sandi Mann and Rebekah Cadman's study on the relationship between boredom and creativity is found in:

'Does Being Bored Make Us More Creative?'
Source: *Creativity Research Journal, vol. 26, no. 2, 2014*

Chapter 3

The idea of failing quickly and cheaply has been around for a while. I first heard about it from technology entrepreneur and speaker Mick Luibinskis.

Information on WD-40 was from:

'John S. Barry, Main Force Behind WD-40, Dies at 84'
Source: *New York Times*

Chapter 4

Some of the ideas and concepts in this chapter appear in my book *Umm...a Complete Guide to Public Speaking* (Allen & Unwin) and/or have been developed from various pitching and public speaking workshops I have conducted.

Chapter 5

Some of the ideas and concepts in this chapter appear in my previous books and articles, particularly *How to Balance your Life* (Allen & Unwin).

Chapter 7

Information about Google's 20 per cent innovation time was found at:

'Google's staff now too busy for 20% time off perk, claim former employees'

Source: *Daily Mail Australia*

'Google's Best New Innovation: Rules Around "20% Time"'

Source: *Forbes,* http://www.20timeineducation.com/

'Google's "20 percent time" in action'

Source: *Google Official Blog*

ACKNOWLEDGEMENTS

Leanne Christie made me do it! Leanne encouraged me to write this book, and kept at it until I agreed to do it. She is a big-hearted powerhouse who is full of great advice. Thanks! Thank you to everyone else at Ode Management, especially those who helped me with many of the ideas that appear in this book, including Heidi Gregory, Lauren Kelly, Julie Winterbottom and Fiona Pascoe.

Thanks to Phil Ryan and my father Graham for reading an early draft and providing helpful and excellent feedback that didn't make me cry. Many of their suggestions have been incorporated into the book.

Thanks to the wonderful Lucy Raymond at Wiley for being receptive to the idea and full of terrific suggestions that have helped to shape this book. Jem Bates did a wonderful job editing the manuscript, and his suggestions were clever, helpful and improved the book no end.

Good on you, Matthew Martin. It's not that hard to come up with a cover illustration that shows the *products* of innovation, but we wanted something that showed the *process* of innovation, and that's really hard. But you nailed it!

Colin James helped me fashion my thoughts on innovation, and guided me when I wasn't sure where I was going. He always seemed to know what the right direction was.

Thanks also to Lisa McInnes-Smith and Dan Gregory for excellent advice, and to Andrew Taylor for so much assistance over many years.

Thanks to the ABC and especially to all those responsible for putting *The New Inventors* on, giving me the opportunity to host it, and keeping it on for eight years. Thanks to all the wonderful producers, researchers, production assistants and crew who worked on the show, and a special mention to Pascal Adolphe and Stewart Burchmore, who were there for the whole eight years. Thanks also to all *The New Inventors* judges, whose insights added to my store of knowledge and whose friendship added to my store of . . . well, friendship.

Thanks to John O'Brien for giving me the opportunity to be involved with the Australian Cleantech Competition, later the Australian Technologies Competition. John is a great champion of Australian innovation.

Thanks to all the many organisations and companies I have spoken to and worked with over the years.

And a huge thank you to all the inventors and innovators I have met, worked with and learned from. It's wonderful to meet people whose minds have gone somewhere new, and who have then had the guts and determination to take their idea out into the world. I salute you all!

Finally, as always, thanks to my wife Lucy and children Bibi, Nina and Lily for everything. I salute you too!!

INDEX

Connect
with WILEY ▶▶▶

WILEY

Browse and purchase the full range of Wiley publications on our official website.

www.wiley.com

Check out the Wiley blog for news, articles and information from Wiley and our authors.

www.wileybizaus.com

Join the conversation on Twitter and keep up to date on the latest news and events in business.

@WileyBizAus

Sign up for Wiley newsletters to learn about our latest publications, upcoming events and conferences, and discounts available to our customers.

www.wiley.com/email

Wiley titles are also produced in e-book formats. Available from all good retailers.

WILEY

Learn more with practical advice from our experts